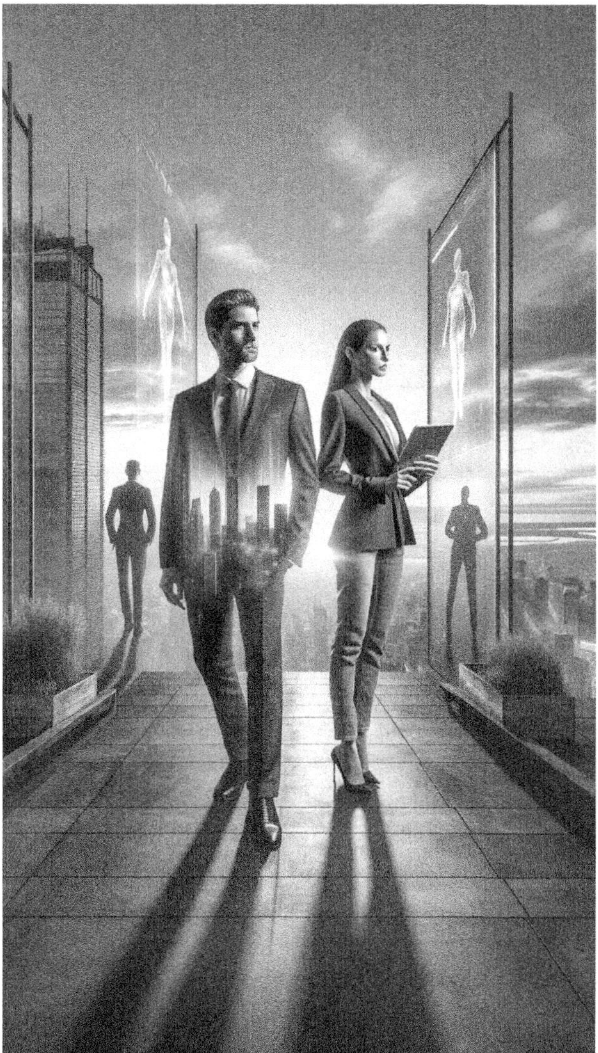

Published by:

Title: Crafting Your Leadership Brand Steps for Crafting Your Leadership Identity To inspire And Influence Others
Author: Patrick S. Muphy
Publisher: Patrick S. Murphy
Publication Date: [March 2024]
ISBN: Genre: Self-Help / Personal Development

Book Description:
A personal leadership brand represents the unique amalgamation of skills, experiences, and values an individual brings to leadership, defining their professional identity and how they're perceived by others. This brand not only mirrors a leader's current style and principles but also their goals for the kind of leader they aspire to be. Crafting a distinct leadership brand is crucial for clarity and direction in one's career, setting one apart in a competitive environment, ensuring consistency in interactions, influencing and inspiring others effectively, and leaving a legacy. It necessitates introspection, continuous feedback, and a dedication to growth, evolving with new experiences and challenges. By deliberately developing their leadership brand, individuals can enhance their professional satisfaction and have a significant impact on their teams and organizations. The importance of a personal leadership brand stems from several key reasons:

Author Bio:
Patrick S. Muphy is a respected leadership expert in the field of personal development and leadership. With a background in leadership training, public speaking, and published author he brings a wealth of experience and insights to the pages of

Contact Information:
For media inquiries, interview requests, or speaking engagements, please contact Patrick S. Murphy at faithmanmurphy@gmail.com

Rights   Information:
For rights inquiries, including translation and international rights, please contact Patrick S. Murphy at faithmanmurphy@gmail.com

Crafting Your Leadership Brand

Steps for Crafting Your Leadership Identity to Inspire And Influence Others

Contents

Establishing Your Personal Leadership Brand: Defining Its Essence and Significance 6

    Fill in the Blank Questions 9

    Multiple Choice Questions 9

    Books: 10

    Additional Resources: 10

Exploring the Impact of a Strong Leadership Brand on Career Advancement, Team Dynamics, and Organizational Success 11

    Career Progression 13

    Team Performance 13

    Organizational Influence 14

    Fill in the Blank Questions 14

    Multiple Choice Questions 15

    Books: 15

Strategies for Identifying Your Core Values, Strengths, and Leadership Qualities 17

    1. Core Values Identification Exercise 19

    2. Strengths Assessment Exercise 19

    3. Leadership Qualities Reflection Exercise 20

    4. Visual Representation Exercise 20

    5. Daily Reflection Journal 20

    Fill in the Blank Questions 21

    Multiple Choice Questions 21

    Books: 22

    Additional Resources: 22

Approaches for Soliciting Feedback on Leadership Style and Perceptions: Tools and Methods 23

    1. 360-Degree Feedback 25

    2. Self-Assessment Tools 26

3. Direct Surveys 26

4. One-on-One Meetings 26

5. Performance Reviews 26

6. Informal Feedback Channels 27

7. Leadership Coaching 27

8. Peer Feedback Groups 27

Utilizing Feedback Effectively 27

Fill in the Blank Questions 28

Multiple Choice Questions 28

Books: 29

Additional Resources: 29

Strategies for Developing a Clear Vision of Your Desired Leadership Identity 31

1. Reflect on Inspirational Leaders 33

2. Define Your Leadership Principles 33

3. Envision Your Future Self 33

4. Set Specific Leadership Goals 34

5. Seek Feedback and Mentorship 34

6. Continuous Learning and Reflection 34

Fill in the Blank Questions 35

Multiple Choice Questions 35

Books: 35

Additional Resources: 36

Aligning Personal and Professional Aspirations: Establishing Short-Term and Long-Term Leadership Goals 37

Short-term Leadership Goals (1-12 months) 39

Long-term Leadership Goals (1-5 years) 40

Examples and Strategies: 40

Setting and Achieving Your Goals 41

Fill in the Blank Questions 41

5

    Multiple Choice Questions...41

    Books: 42

    Additional Resources: 42

Crafting Your Distinctive Leadership Brand Statement: A Step-by-Step Guide 44

    Step 1: Reflect on Your Core Values 46

    Step 2: Acknowledge Your Strengths 46

    Step 3: Clarify Your Leadership Vision...47

    Step 4: Draft Your Leadership Brand Statement 47

    Step 5: Seek Feedback 47

    Step 6: Finalize Your Statement 47

    Step 7: Live Your Leadership Brand 48

    Example of a Leadership Brand Statement 48

    Fill in the Blank Questions..48

    Multiple Choice Questions..48

    Books: 49

    Additional Resources: 49

Effective Examples of Leadership Brand Statements: Inspiring Models for Professional Identity 50

    Fill in the Blank Questions..53

    Multiple Choice Questions..54

    Books: 54

    Additional Resources: 55

Strategies for Strategic Communication: Effectively Transmitting Your Leadership Brand Across Multiple Channels 56

    1. Social Media...58

    2. Professional Networks 58

    3. Personal Interactions 59

    4. Thought Leadership 59

    5. Digital Presence 59

6. Visual Branding 60
Fill in the Blank Questions 60
Multiple Choice Questions 60
Books: 61
Additional Resources: 61

The Significance of Consistency in Verbal and Non-Verbal Communication: Strengthening Your Leadership Brand 62
Verbal Communication 64
Non-Verbal Communication 64
Building Trust and Credibility 65
Enhancing Leadership Presence 65
Fill in the Blank Questions: 66
Multiple Choice Questions: 66
Books: 66
Additional Resources: 67

Ensuring Alignment: Tips for Reflecting Your Leadership Brand and Core Values in Daily Actions and Interactions 68
1. Start with Self-Awareness 70
2. Set Clear Intentions 70
3. Practice Consistency 70
4. Lead by Example 71
5. Adapt and Evolve 71
6. Foster Relationships 71
7. Reflect and Adjust 71
Fill in the Blank: 72
Multiple Choice: 72
Books: 73
Additional Resources: 73

Embracing Authenticity and Integrity: Pillars of Living Your Leadership Brand 74

- Authenticity 76
- Integrity 76
- Living Your Leadership Brand with Authenticity and Integrity 77
- Fill in the Blank: 77
- Multiple Choice: 78
- Books: 78
- Additional Resources: 79

Building Your Professional Network: Guidance for Expanding and Nurturing a Supportive Ecosystem for Your Leadership Brand 80

- 1. Identify Your Networking Goals 82
- 2. Leverage LinkedIn and Other Professional Platforms 82
- 3. Attend Industry Events and Conferences 83
- 4. Create and Share Valuable Content 83
- 5. Foster Genuine Connections 83
- 6. Seek Out and Provide Mentorship 83
- 7. Engage in Continuous Learning and Development 84
- 8. Utilize Social Media Wisely 84
- 9. Give Back to Your Community 84
- 10. Be Patient and Persistent 84
- Fill in the Blank: 85
- Multiple Choice: 85
- Books: 85
- Additional Resources: 86

Unlocking Leadership Potential: Harnessing Mentorship for Personal Growth and Development 87

- As a Mentee 88
- As a Mentor 89
- Maximizing the Benefits of Mentorship 90
- Fill in the Blank: 90
- Multiple Choice: 90

Books: 91
Additional Resources: 91

Embracing Lifelong Learning: Strategies for Evolving Your Leadership Brand Over Time 93

1. Embrace a Growth Mindset 95
2. Set Learning Goals 95
3. Leverage Formal Education and Training 96
4. Utilize Online Resources 96
5. Engage in Peer Learning 96
6. Read Widely 96
7. Reflect and Apply 97
8. Stay Informed on Global Trends 97
9. Network and Collaborate 97
10. Prioritize Self-Care 97
Fill in the Blank: 98
Multiple Choice: 98
Books: 98
Additional Resources: 99

Embracing Feedback and Adaptation: Keys to Effective Leadership Evolution 100

Fill in the Blank: 103
Multiple Choice: 104
Additional Resources: 105

Navigating Challenges in Leadership Brand Development: Strategies for Success 106

1. Lack of Clarity 108
2. Consistency Issues 108
3. Evolving Leadership Context 108
4. Feedback Integration 108
5. Visibility 109

6. Balancing Authenticity and Adaptability 109

7. Building Trust 109

8. Differentiation 109

Fill in the Blank: 110

Multiple Choice: 110

Books: 111

Additional Resources: 111

Navigating Obstacles: Case Studies of Leaders Strengthening Their Leadership Brand Through Adversity 112

1. Satya Nadella - Microsoft 114

2. Indra Nooyi - PepsiCo 114

3. Howard Schultz - Starbucks 114

4. Mary Barra - General Motors 115

Fill in the Blank: 115

Multiple Choice: 116

Books: 116

Additional Resources: 117

Evaluating Leadership Brand Effectiveness: Methods for Personal, Team, and Organizational Assessment 118

1. 360-Degree Feedback 120

2. Self-Assessment Tools 120

3. Performance Metrics 121

4. Employee Engagement Surveys 121

5. Professional Development Milestones 121

6. Observation of Team Dynamics 121

7. Organizational Culture Assessments 122

8. Mentor and Peer Review 122

Fill in the Blank: 122

Multiple Choice: 123

Books: 123

Additional Resources: 124

Tools for Feedback and Progress Measurement: Enhancing Leadership Development Journey 125

1. 360-Degree Feedback Tools 127
2. Performance Review Platforms..127
3. Employee Engagement Surveys..127
4. Goal Tracking Software 128
5. Professional Development Platforms 128
6. Feedback Apps 128
7. Journaling and Reflection Apps 128
8. Peer Learning and Mentorship Platforms 129
Fill in the Blank:...129
Multiple Choice:...129
Additional Resources: 130

Embracing Leadership Brand Evolution: Encouragement for Dynamic Professional Identity Growth...............................132

Fill in the Blank:...135
Multiple Choice:...135
Books: 136
Additional Resources: 136
5 Years Later:..139

Resource Toolkit: Templates and Worksheets for Leadership Brand Development Exercises 142

1. Core Values Identification Worksheet 142
2. Strengths and Leadership Qualities Assessment Template.....142
3. Leadership Vision Statement Guide....................................143
4. Feedback Collection Form 143
5. Personal Development Plan Template 143
6. 360-Degree Feedback Analysis Worksheet 144

Introduction

Establishing Your Personal Leadership Brand: Defining Its Essence and Significance

In the metropolis of Futureville, where the skyline was a jagged line of gleaming towers and innovation thrived at every corner, there lived a young leader named Alex Carver. Alex was an ambitious project manager at InnovateTech, a company known for breaking boundaries in technology. Despite Alex's successes, they felt something was missing. They yearned to not just lead but inspire, to not only direct but empower. This is the story of how Alex crafted a personal leadership brand that transformed not just their career, but the lives of those they led.

Alex's journey began on a typical Monday morning, amidst the chaos of back-to-back meetings and a never-ending stream of emails. Amidst the hustle, a question from a new team member, Jamie, caught Alex off guard. "How would you describe your leadership style?" Jamie asked innocently. Alex was stumped. They had never really thought about it. That evening, sitting in the quiet of their sleek, minimally furnished apartment, Alex pondered over Jamie's question. It dawned on them that without a clear leadership identity, they were just another face in the crowd of managers.

Determined to change, Alex embarked on a journey of introspection. They reflected on their skills, experiences, and values. Alex realized their strength lay in empathy and innovation, having led several successful projects by understanding the team's needs and pushing the boundaries of what was possible. They valued integrity, inclusivity, and growth, both for themselves and their team. But Alex wanted more; they aspired to be a leader who not only achieved goals but inspired their team to see beyond the daily tasks, to innovate and strive for a better future.

Armed with this self-awareness, Alex sought continuous feedback from peers, mentors, and team members. They embraced the critiques and praises, seeing them as building blocks for their leadership brand. Alex began to make changes, focusing on clear communication, fostering a culture of innovation, and being more accessible to their team. They started sharing their vision and goals, not just for projects but for what the team could collectively achieve.

Alex's dedication to growth and evolution became the cornerstone of their leadership brand. They attended workshops, read extensively, and even started a mentorship program within InnovateTech to support emerging leaders. Alex's brand was not static; it evolved with every new challenge and experience, staying relevant and inspiring.

The impact of Alex's deliberate development of their leadership brand was profound. Team members were more engaged, innovation thrived, and projects exceeded expectations. Alex's brand of leadership became synonymous with integrity, innovation, and inspiration. Their approach influenced not just their team but other leaders within InnovateTech, sparking a shift towards a more inclusive and visionary leadership style.

Years later, as Alex moved on to larger roles and greater challenges, their leadership brand left a legacy within InnovateTech. New leaders spoke of Alex's influence, of the culture of innovation and empowerment they fostered. Alex's journey from a project manager to a visionary leader underscored the importance of crafting a personal leadership brand. It was not just about leading efficiently but leading in a way that inspired change, fostered growth, and made a lasting impact.

Through introspection, feedback, and a commitment to growth, Alex demonstrated that a personal leadership brand is not a static label but a dynamic, evolving identity that shapes not just a career but the lives of those one leads. In the competitive environment of Futureville, Alex Carver stood out not just for what they achieved but for who they were as a leader.

A personal leadership brand represents the unique amalgamation of skills, experiences, and values an individual brings to leadership, defining their professional identity and how they're perceived by others. This brand not only mirrors a leader's current style and principles but also their goals for the kind of leader they aspire to be. Crafting a distinct leadership brand is crucial for clarity and direction in one's career, setting one apart in a competitive environment, ensuring consistency in interactions, influencing and inspiring others effectively, and leaving a legacy. It necessitates introspection, continuous feedback, and a dedication to growth, evolving with new experiences and challenges. By deliberately developing their leadership brand, individuals can enhance their professional satisfaction and have a significant impact on their teams and organizations. The importance of a personal leadership brand stems from several key reasons:

1. **Clarity and Direction**: It helps you to clarify your personal and professional goals, providing a sense of direction in your leadership journey. This clarity guides your decisions and actions, ensuring they are aligned with your core values and the outcomes you wish to achieve.
2. **Differentiation**: In a competitive professional environment, having a distinct leadership brand sets you apart from others. It highlights your unique strengths and capabilities, making you more memorable and valued in your organization and industry.
3. **Consistency**: A well-defined leadership brand ensures consistency in how you present yourself and interact with others. Consistency builds trust and credibility, as people know what to expect from you and can rely on you to be true to your word.
4. **Influence and Impact**: Your leadership brand affects how you influence and inspire those around you. A strong, positive brand can motivate your team, foster loyalty, and drive better performance, contributing to the overall success of your organization.
5. **Legacy**: Ultimately, your leadership brand contributes to the legacy you leave behind. It reflects the difference you've made in your professional sphere and the lasting impression you leave on your colleagues and the organization as a whole.

Developing and cultivating a personal leadership brand requires introspection, feedback, and a commitment to personal growth and development. It's an ongoing process that evolves as you gain more experience and face new challenges. By intentionally shaping your leadership brand, you can achieve greater professional fulfillment and make a meaningful impact on those you lead.

Fill in the Blank Questions

1. A personal leadership brand encapsulates an individual's _____, experiences, and values.
2. Developing a personal leadership brand requires _____, feedback, and a commitment to personal growth.
3. A well-defined leadership brand ensures _____ in how you present yourself and interact with others.
4. Your leadership brand contributes to the _____ you leave behind in your professional sphere.

Multiple Choice Questions

1. **What does a personal leadership brand represent?**
   A) A leader's salary expectations
   B) The unique combination of skills, experiences, and values a leader brings
   C) Only the professional achievements of a leader
   D) The leader's personal hobbies and interests
2. **Why is having a distinct leadership brand important?**
   A) It ensures a higher salary.
   B) It sets one apart in a competitive environment.
   C) It is required for all leadership positions.
   D) It simplifies leadership responsibilities.
3. **What does a well-defined leadership brand contribute to?**
   A) Decreased team performance
   B) The legacy a leader leaves behind
   C) Reduced influence on others
   D) Increased operational costs
4. **Developing and cultivating a personal leadership brand is described as:**
   A) A one-time task upon achieving a leadership position

B) Only necessary for new leaders
C) An ongoing process that evolves with experience
D) Less important than other leadership tasks

Books:

1. **"Leadership Brand: Developing Customer-Focused Leaders to Drive Performance and Build Lasting Value"** by Dave Ulrich and Norm Smallwood - Explores the concept of leadership branding and provides practical guidance on how to develop and leverage a personal leadership brand to drive organizational success.
2. **"The Leadership Challenge: How to Make Extraordinary Things Happen in Organizations"** by James M. Kouzes and Barry Z. Posner - Discusses the fundamental principles of effective leadership and offers insights into how individuals can cultivate their own leadership brand through exemplary practices.
3. **"Personal Branding for Dummies"** by Susan Chritton - Although not specifically focused on leadership, this book offers valuable insights into personal branding principles that can be applied to leadership development, including defining one's unique value proposition and managing perceptions effectively.

Additional Resources:

1. **Harvard Business Review** articles on personal branding and leadership development - HBR provides numerous articles on leadership and personal branding, offering research-based insights and practical tips for individuals looking to craft their own leadership brand.
2. Online courses on leadership branding and personal development on platforms like **SkillPath**, **Coursera**, **LinkedIn Learning**, and **Udemy** - These platforms offer a variety of courses taught by industry experts that delve into topics such as personal branding, leadership development, and self-awareness, providing actionable strategies for individuals to enhance their leadership brand.

3. **Podcasts** and **TED Talks** featuring thought leaders in the field of leadership and personal branding - Listening to podcasts and TED Talks can provide inspiration and fresh perspectives on leadership development and personal branding, offering practical advice and real-life examples from successful leaders.

Exploring the Impact of a Strong Leadership Brand on Career Advancement, Team Dynamics, and Organizational Success

As Alex's leadership brand grew stronger, so did their influence within InnovateTech and beyond. They became a beacon of visionary leadership, not just within their team but across the entire organization. Alex's clear communication of their brand and its alignment with their actions led to a noticeable enhancement in their career progression. Opportunities that once seemed distant dreams became realities—leading larger projects, speaking at industry conferences, and eventually, a well-deserved promotion to a senior leadership role.

Alex's leadership brand, characterized by empathy, innovation, and a commitment to growth, resonated deeply within their team. It fostered an environment of trust and motivation, where team members felt valued and understood. This cohesion was palpable in team meetings, project collaborations, and the way challenges were approached—not as obstacles but as opportunities for innovation. The team's performance soared, not just in terms of project outcomes but in their ability to inspire and influence other teams within InnovateTech. They were setting new standards for what was possible, driven by a shared commitment to Alex's vision and values.

At an organizational level, Alex's leadership brand became a powerful tool for change management. Their approach to leadership, which emphasized innovation and inclusivity, aligned perfectly with

InnovateTech's strategic goals. As the company navigated the challenges of rapid growth and technological change, Alex was at the forefront, guiding their team and influencing their peers. They played a crucial role in driving innovation, not just through their projects but by nurturing talent and encouraging a culture of continuous learning and improvement.

Alex's impact extended beyond immediate project successes. They were leaving a legacy within InnovateTech, one that would influence the organization for years to come. By promoting a leadership style that valued innovation and empathy, Alex was helping to shape the next generation of leaders at InnovateTech. Their mentorship program, initially started as a small initiative, grew into a company-wide platform for leadership development. Through this program, Alex was not just sharing their knowledge but empowering others to develop their unique leadership brands, fostering a diverse and dynamic leadership culture within the organization.

The benefits of Alex's strong leadership brand were evident. They enjoyed greater job satisfaction, knowing that their work was not just about achieving business outcomes but about making a real difference in the lives of their team members and shaping the future of InnovateTech. Their career advancement was a testament to the power of a well-defined and communicated leadership brand. But more than the promotions and accolades, what truly mattered to Alex was the trust and respect they had earned from their colleagues, the performance and cohesion of their team, and the positive change they had initiated at an organizational level.

Ultimately, Alex's journey underscored the transformative power of a robust leadership brand. It served as a catalyst for sustained success, benefiting not just Alex but their team, InnovateTech, and the broader industry. By developing and consistently living their leadership brand, Alex had set themselves apart in a competitive environment, leading with integrity, inspiring innovation, and leaving a legacy that would inspire future leaders for years to come.

A strong leadership brand significantly enhances career progression, team performance, and organizational influence. By developing and consistently communicating their leadership brand, leaders gain visibility and recognition, setting them apart in competitive environments and leading to greater job satisfaction and career advancement opportunities. Such a brand fosters trust, motivation, and cohesion within teams, enhancing performance through a shared commitment to clear vision and values. At the organizational level, a well-defined leadership brand aligns with strategic goals, facilitates effective change management, and leaves a legacy by driving innovation and nurturing talent. Ultimately, a robust leadership brand serves as a catalyst for sustained success, benefiting individuals, teams, and the entire organization.

Career Progression

1. **Visibility and Recognition**: Leaders with a clear and compelling leadership brand are more likely to be noticed and recognized by senior management and key stakeholders. This visibility can open doors to new opportunities, promotions, and career advancements.
2. **Differentiation**: In a competitive job market, a well-defined leadership brand helps individuals stand out. It highlights their unique contributions and capabilities, making them more attractive to potential employers or for internal promotions.
3. **Personal Fulfillment**: A leadership brand that aligns with an individual's values and strengths leads to greater job satisfaction and engagement. This fulfillment can drive higher performance, further accelerating career progression.

Team Performance

1. **Trust and Reliability**: Teams led by individuals with a strong leadership brand tend to have higher levels of trust in their leader. This trust stems from the leader's consistency in actions and decisions, which align with their communicated brand.
2. **Motivation and Engagement**: Leaders who effectively communicate their vision and values can inspire and motivate their teams. A clear leadership brand that resonates with the

team's goals and aspirations can enhance engagement and commitment to shared objectives.
3. **Culture and Cohesion**: A strong leadership brand can contribute to a positive team culture, one that values transparency, accountability, and collaboration. By setting the tone through their leadership brand, leaders can foster a cohesive and high-performing team environment.

Organizational Influence

1. **Strategic Alignment**: Leaders with a strong brand that aligns with the organization's mission and values can significantly influence strategic direction. Their clear vision and steadfast commitment can guide decision-making processes and organizational priorities.
2. **Change Management**: In times of change, leaders with a well-established leadership brand are better positioned to steer their teams and the organization through transitions. Their credibility and authority make them effective change agents, capable of overcoming resistance and garnering support for new initiatives.
3. **Legacy and Impact**: Over the long term, a leader's brand contributes to their legacy within the organization. Leaders known for fostering growth, driving innovation, and nurturing talent can leave a lasting impact that shapes the organization's future success and culture.

In summary, a strong leadership brand is not just a personal asset; it's a catalyst for broader organizational success. It enhances the leader's career trajectory, elevates team performance, and extends their influence across the organization, contributing to a sustainable competitive advantage.

Fill in the Blank Questions

1. A strong leadership brand enhances career progression, team performance, and _____ influence.
2. Leaders with a clear and compelling leadership brand gain visibility and _____.

3. A leadership brand that aligns with an individual's values and strengths leads to greater job _____.
4. Leaders known for fostering growth and driving innovation can leave a lasting _____ within the organization.

Multiple Choice Questions

1. **How does a strong leadership brand affect an individual's career?**
   A) Limits career progression
   B) Reduces job satisfaction
   C) Opens doors to new opportunities and advancements
   D) Decreases visibility and recognition
2. **What is a key benefit of a strong leadership brand on team performance?**
   A) Decreases team trust
   B) Enhances motivation and engagement
   C) Reduces team cohesion
   D) Increases team conflicts
3. **Which of the following is an impact of a strong leadership brand at the organizational level?**
   A) Difficulty in managing change
   B) Misalignment with organizational values
   C) Contributes to a lasting legacy and success
   D) Decreases strategic alignment

Books:

1. **"Leaders Eat Last: Why Some Teams Pull Together and Others Don't"** by Simon Sinek - Explores the importance of leadership in fostering trust and collaboration within teams, emphasizing the role of leaders in creating a culture of safety and belonging.
2. **"The Leadership Pipeline: How to Build the Leadership-Powered Company"** by Ram Charan, Stephen Drotter, and James Noel - Discusses the importance of developing leadership capabilities at all levels of an organization and provides practical frameworks for building a strong leadership pipeline.

3. **"Building the Leadership Brand"** by Dave Ulrich and Norm Smallwood - Focuses specifically on the concept of leadership branding and provides insights into how leaders can develop and communicate their brand effectively to drive organizational success.

Chapter 1: Self-Assessment and Reflection

Strategies for Identifying Your Core Values, Strengths, and Leadership Qualities

Inspired by their success and the impact of their leadership brand, Alex decided to deepen their understanding and commitment to personal growth. They embarked on a more structured journey to refine their leadership brand, recognizing that the journey of a leader is never complete but a continuous process of evolution and adaptation.

Alex started with the fundamentals—identifying their core values, strengths, and leadership qualities. They dedicated a weekend to solitude and reflection in a quiet retreat outside Futureville, surrounded by nature, where the hustle of city life felt a world away. Here, Alex engaged in various exercises designed to peel back the layers of their professional persona, revealing the core of their leadership identity.

First, they listed their values, laying them out on paper like pieces of a puzzle waiting to be solved. Integrity, innovation, empathy, inclusivity, and growth emerged as the top priorities. Alex took time to reflect on each value, recalling moments in their career when these values were challenged and how they responded, reinforcing their importance.

Next, Alex took several strength assessments, comparing the results with feedback received from peers, mentors, and team members over the years. This exercise highlighted strengths they were aware of, such as strategic thinking and empathy, but also revealed new areas like resilience and adaptability, which had been crucial in navigating recent challenges at InnovateTech.

Reflecting on leadership stories was particularly enlightening for Alex. They journaled about moments when their leadership made a difference—the launch of a breakthrough project, mentoring a struggling team member, navigating the team through a crisis. These stories not only highlighted consistent leadership qualities but also moments of growth and learning.

Creating a vision board was a new and exciting exercise for Alex. They gathered images, quotes, and symbols representing their aspirations—not just career goals, but the kind of leader they aspired to be, the impact they wished to have, and the legacy they aimed to leave. This visual representation served as a powerful daily reminder of their journey and goals.

Maintaining a daily reflection journal became part of Alex's routine. Each evening, they would spend a few minutes reflecting on the day—challenges faced, successes achieved, and lessons learned. This practice fostered ongoing self-awareness and personal growth, allowing Alex to see the gradual evolution of their leadership brand in real-time.

Engaging regularly with these exercises ensured that Alex's leadership brand remained dynamic, aligning with their evolving leadership journey. It was a process that demanded honesty, vulnerability, and a commitment to growth, but Alex found it incredibly rewarding. It not only deepened their understanding of themselves as a leader but also enhanced their ability to lead with authenticity, inspire their team, and drive meaningful change within InnovateTech.

Through this introspective journey, Alex's leadership brand became more nuanced and powerful. It was a true reflection of who they were and who they aspired to become, embodying their values, strengths, and vision for the future. This alignment between personal identity and professional persona made Alex not just a leader but a beacon of inspiration and change, embodying the essence of a personal leadership brand.

Identifying your core values, strengths, and leadership qualities is fundamental to developing a personal leadership brand. Exercises such as listing and prioritizing your values, taking strength assessments, reflecting on leadership stories, creating a vision board, and maintaining a daily reflection journal can significantly aid in this discovery process. These activities help in pinpointing the values you won't compromise on, understanding your unique strengths through feedback and self-analysis, and identifying consistent leadership qualities through personal stories. A vision board can visually represent your aspirations, while a daily journal fosters ongoing self-awareness and personal growth. Regular engagement with these exercises ensures your leadership brand remains aligned with your evolving leadership journey, making them crucial for continuous development and alignment with your personal leadership brand.

1. Core Values Identification Exercise

- **List Your Values**: Start by listing out values that resonate with you. Don't overthink it; write down all the values that come to mind.
- **Narrow Down**: From your list, choose the top 5 values that you feel most strongly about. These are values you cannot compromise on, regardless of the situation.
- **Reflect and Validate**: For each core value, reflect on a past situation where this value guided your decision-making. This helps validate that these values are indeed core to your being.

2. Strengths Assessment Exercise

- **StrengthsFinder Assessment**: Taking a formal assessment like Gallup's Clifton Strengths can provide insight into your dominant themes of talent and areas of strength.
- **Feedback Analysis**: Ask colleagues, friends, and mentors for feedback on your strengths. Look for patterns in what others perceive as your strengths.
- **Reflect on Successes**: Think about moments of success and satisfaction in your professional life. What strengths were you

using? Identifying these can help you understand your unique strengths better.

3. Leadership Qualities Reflection Exercise

- **Leadership Stories**: Write down three to five stories from your life where you felt you effectively led others. These can be from any context, not just professional.
- **Analyze for Qualities**: For each story, identify the leadership qualities you exhibited that contributed to the success of the situation.
- **Consolidation**: Look for patterns across the stories to pinpoint your consistent leadership qualities.

4. Visual Representation Exercise

- **Create a Vision Board**: Use images, words, and symbols to create a vision board that represents your core values, strengths, and leadership qualities. This visual representation can serve as a daily reminder of who you aspire to be as a leader.

5. Daily Reflection Journal

- **Keep a Daily Journal**: Dedicate a few minutes at the end of each day to reflect on how you demonstrated your core values, utilized your strengths, and embodied your leadership qualities. This practice can reinforce self-awareness and guide personal growth.

These exercises are not one-time tasks but ongoing processes that can evolve as you grow and develop in your leadership journey. Regularly revisiting and reassessing your core values, strengths, and leadership qualities is essential for maintaining alignment with your personal leadership brand.

Fill in the Blank Questions

1. Identifying your core values, strengths, and leadership qualities is fundamental to developing a personal _____ brand.
2. Taking a formal assessment like Gallup's Clifton Strengths can provide insight into your dominant themes of _____ and areas of strength.
3. A vision board can visually represent your core values, strengths, and leadership qualities, serving as a daily reminder of who you aspire to be as a _____.
4. Maintaining a daily _____ journal helps foster ongoing self-awareness and guides personal growth.

Multiple Choice Questions

1. What is the purpose of listing and prioritizing your values in developing a personal leadership brand?
A) To decide on your next job position
B) To identify values you cannot compromise on
C) To share them on social media
D) To compare them with your friends' values

2. What can taking strength assessments help you understand?
A) Your financial investments
B) Your dominant themes of talent and areas of strength
C) Your favorite hobbies
D) Your educational background

3. Why create a vision board in the context of leadership development?
A) To plan your next vacation
B) To represent your core values, strengths, and leadership qualities visually
C) To decorate your room
D) To pass time

4. What does maintaining a daily reflection journal aid in?
A) Tracking daily expenses
B) Fostering ongoing self-awareness and personal growth

C) Planning your meals
D) Remembering birthdays

Books:

1. **"Dare to Lead: Brave Work. Tough Conversations. Whole Hearts."** by Brené Brown - This book explores the importance of courage, vulnerability, and values-based leadership. Brown provides practical exercises and insights to help readers identify their core values and develop their leadership qualities.
2. **"StrengthsFinder 2.0"** by Tom Rath - Based on Gallup's research, this book offers an assessment tool to identify individuals' top strengths and provides strategies for leveraging these strengths in leadership roles.
3. **"The Leadership Challenge: How to Make Extraordinary Things Happen in Organizations"** by James M. Kouzes and Barry Z. Posner - This classic book presents a framework for effective leadership and includes exercises to help readers identify their leadership values and qualities.

Additional Resources:

1. **Values Clarification Exercises** - Various online resources and worksheets are available to guide individuals through the process of identifying and prioritizing their core values. Websites like MindTools offer free tools and exercises for values clarification.
2. **Leadership Stories Reflection Guide** - Templates and prompts for reflecting on personal leadership stories can be found in leadership development books, online forums, and leadership training materials. These resources help individuals identify consistent leadership qualities and strengths demonstrated in past experiences.
3. **Vision Board Creation Guides** - Websites like Canva provide templates and tutorials for creating vision boards digitally. Additionally, books on visualization techniques and personal development often include guidance on creating vision boards as a tool for clarifying goals and aspirations.

4. **Daily Reflection Journal Prompts** - Numerous journals and online resources offer daily prompts for reflection and self-awareness. Websites like Greater Good Magazine and Tiny Buddha provide articles with reflection prompts and exercises aimed at personal growth and development.

Approaches for Soliciting Feedback on Leadership Style and Perceptions: Tools and Methods

Motivated by their recent self-discovery and the enhancement of their leadership brand, Alex turned their attention to the next critical step: gathering and analyzing feedback on their leadership style and perception. They recognized that understanding how they were perceived by others was crucial for their continuous development as a leader. This phase was about bridging the gap between self-perception and external perception, ensuring their leadership brand was not only authentic to themselves but also resonated effectively with others.

Alex began with the implementation of a 360-Degree Feedback process at InnovateTech. They worked with the HR department to design and distribute the feedback forms, ensuring anonymity to encourage honest and constructive feedback. This tool would provide a well-rounded view of Alex's leadership from peers, subordinates, and clients.

Concurrently, Alex engaged in Self-Assessment Tools, including the Myers-Briggs Type Indicator (MBTI). This assessment provided deeper insights into their personality traits and how these traits influenced their leadership style. Understanding their MBTI type helped Alex recognize their natural strengths and areas where they could improve their approach to leading others.

Direct Surveys were another method Alex used to gather specific feedback. They designed surveys with targeted questions about various aspects of their leadership, such as decision-making processes, communication effectiveness, and ability to inspire and motivate the team. This approach allowed Alex to collect actionable insights that could be directly applied to enhance their leadership effectiveness.

One-on-One Meetings became a regular part of Alex's schedule. These meetings were not just about project updates or performance reviews but also offered a platform for team members to share their perceptions and experiences of Alex's leadership in a more personal and direct manner.

Through Performance Reviews and Informal Feedback Channels, Alex received additional insights. They paid close attention to comments related to their leadership during team performance discussions, and they encouraged an open-door policy where team members could share their thoughts and suggestions informally.

To further deepen their understanding and development, Alex engaged in Leadership Coaching. Working with a coach provided personalized insights into their leadership style, helping Alex to identify blind spots and areas for improvement that they might not have noticed on their own. Additionally, Alex joined a Peer Feedback Group, consisting of leaders from different departments within InnovateTech. This group met monthly, sharing challenges and feedback in a supportive environment, offering diverse perspectives and fostering a culture of continuous improvement.

Effectively utilizing the feedback involved meticulous analysis to identify common themes and actionable insights. Alex dedicated time to reflect on this feedback, comparing it against their self-assessment and the objectives of their leadership brand. This process was eye-opening; it highlighted areas of strength, such as empathy and strategic vision, and areas for improvement, such as delegating more effectively and managing stress under tight deadlines.

This feedback loop underscored the importance of openness to change and a commitment to continuous improvement. Alex realized that leadership development was an ongoing journey, requiring humility, resilience, and the willingness to adapt and grow.

By actively seeking out and utilizing feedback, Alex not only enhanced their leadership brand but also reinforced their effectiveness as a leader. They became more attuned to the needs and perceptions of their team, leading with greater awareness and impact.

Through these concerted efforts, Alex's leadership brand evolved into a dynamic and impactful force within InnovateTech. It was a brand built on self-awareness, continuous feedback, and an unwavering commitment to personal and professional growth. Alex's journey demonstrated that effective leadership is not just about leading with authority but about inspiring with authenticity, understanding, and adaptability.

Gathering feedback on your leadership style and perception is essential for any leader's development. Tools like 360-Degree Feedback provide anonymous insights from peers, subordinates, and sometimes clients, while Self-Assessment Tools such as the Myers-Briggs Type Indicator (MBTI) help leaders understand their personality traits and strengths. Direct Surveys offer a way to gather specific feedback on various aspects of leadership, and One-on-One Meetings allow for in-depth conversations. Performance Reviews and Informal Feedback Channels are also valuable for receiving feedback, not only about your team's performance but also about your leadership impact. Additionally, Leadership Coaching and Peer Feedback Groups provide personalized insights and peer perspectives. Effectively utilizing this feedback involves analyzing it to identify common themes and areas for improvement, thereby enhancing your leadership brand and effectiveness. The process underscores the importance of openness to change and a commitment to continuous improvement in leadership development.

1. 360-Degree Feedback

- **Description**: A comprehensive feedback process where leaders receive confidential, anonymous feedback from the people who work around them. This typically includes peers, direct reports, managers, and sometimes clients.

- **Implementation**: Utilize a formal 360-degree feedback tool or service that offers standardized surveys to collect and analyze feedback on various leadership competencies.

2. Self-Assessment Tools

- **Description**: Tools like the Myers-Briggs Type Indicator (MBTI) or the StrengthsFinder can help leaders gain insight into their personality traits, strengths, and potential areas for improvement.
- **Implementation**: Complete these assessments and compare your self-perception with the feedback from others to identify gaps or confirmations in your leadership style.

3. Direct Surveys

- **Description**: Customized surveys sent directly to team members or peers to gather specific feedback on your leadership practices, communication style, decision-making process, and more.
- **Implementation**: Use online survey tools like SurveyMonkey or Google Forms to design and distribute your surveys, ensuring anonymity to get honest responses.

4. One-on-One Meetings

- **Description**: Personal, direct conversations with team members and peers can provide in-depth feedback and insights into your leadership style.
- **Implementation**: Schedule regular one-on-one meetings with an open agenda to encourage honest communication. Prepare specific questions to guide the conversation towards feedback on your leadership.

5. Performance Reviews

- **Description**: Regularly scheduled performance reviews can be a source of feedback, not just for the employee being reviewed but also for the leader conducting the review.

- **Implementation**: During these reviews, ask for feedback on your leadership style and how it impacts the team member's work and motivation.

6. Informal Feedback Channels

- **Description**: Creating an environment that encourages informal feedback can provide insights into how your leadership style is perceived daily.
- **Implementation**: Foster a culture where team members feel comfortable sharing feedback spontaneously. Be approachable, and show appreciation for feedback received, regardless of the formality of the setting.

7. Leadership Coaching

- **Description**: Working with a leadership coach can offer personalized insights into your leadership style. Coaches can also act as intermediaries to collect feedback on your behalf.
- **Implementation**: Engage a coach who can observe you in action, collect feedback from colleagues and direct reports, and provide you with a structured analysis and improvement plan.

8. Peer Feedback Groups

- **Description**: Participating in or forming a peer feedback group with other leaders can offer valuable perspectives on your leadership style from those in similar roles.
- **Implementation**: Organize regular meetings with a trusted group of peers to exchange feedback on leadership challenges, strategies, and personal growth areas.

Utilizing Feedback Effectively

Once you've collected feedback, it's crucial to analyze the data thoughtfully, identify common themes, and develop a plan for addressing any areas for improvement. Remember, the goal of gathering feedback is not just to affirm what you're doing well but to uncover areas where you can grow and develop as a leader. Openness to change and a commitment to continuous improvement are key to leveraging feedback to enhance your leadership brand and effectiveness.

Fill in the Blank Questions

1. The _____-Degree Feedback process involves receiving anonymous feedback from peers, direct reports, and managers.
2. Tools like the Myers-Briggs Type Indicator (MBTI) are used for _____-assessment to understand a leader's personality traits.
3. _____ Surveys can be customized and sent to team members to gather feedback on leadership practices.
4. Leadership _____ can provide personalized insights and act as intermediaries to collect feedback.

Multiple Choice Questions

1. What is the purpose of 360-Degree Feedback?
A) To evaluate employee performance
B) To provide leaders with anonymous feedback from their work circle
C) To assess client satisfaction
D) To measure financial success

2. How can leaders use Self-Assessment Tools?
A) To plan team outings
B) To understand their strengths and areas for improvement
C) To calculate budgets
D) To schedule meetings

3. What is the benefit of Direct Surveys in gathering leadership feedback?
A) They provide a platform for anonymous, specific feedback
B) They are only used for marketing purposes
C) They help in organizing events
D) They track sales performance

4. Which of the following is a method for receiving in-depth feedback?
A) Checking emails
B) One-on-One Meetings
C) Updating software
D) Reading industry magazines

Books:

1. **"Thanks for the Feedback: The Science and Art of Receiving Feedback Well"** by Douglas Stone and Sheila Heen - This book offers practical strategies for receiving feedback effectively and using it to improve in various aspects of life, including leadership.
2. **"Leadership Agility: Five Levels of Mastery for Anticipating and Initiating Change"** by Bill Joiner and Stephen Josephs - This book provides insights into how leaders can develop agility in responding to feedback and adapting their leadership style to meet evolving challenges.
3. **"Coaching for Performance: GROWing Human Potential and Purpose - The Principles and Practice of Coaching and Leadership"** by Sir John Whitmore - This book offers guidance on how leaders can use coaching techniques to enhance their effectiveness, including receiving and giving feedback.

Additional Resources:

1. **360-Degree Feedback Platforms** - Various online platforms like **Qualtrics 360** and **SurveyMonkey** offer customizable surveys for gathering anonymous feedback from multiple sources, including peers, subordinates, and clients.
2. **Self-Assessment Tools** - Websites like the Myers-Briggs Foundation and Gallup offer assessments like the **MBTI** and **StrengthsFinder**, respectively, to help leaders understand their personality traits, strengths, and areas for development.
3. **Leadership Coaching Programs** - Many coaching institutes and individual coaches offer leadership coaching services, providing personalized feedback and guidance tailored to individual leadership development goals.

4. **Peer Feedback Groups** - Joining or forming peer feedback groups allows leaders to receive constructive feedback and support from their peers in a safe and confidential environment. Online platforms like Meetup or LinkedIn groups can facilitate the formation of such groups.
5. **Performance Review Templates** - Websites like Indeed and SHRM provide templates and guidelines for conducting performance reviews, which can be adapted for gathering feedback on leadership impact and effectiveness.
6. **Informal Feedback Channels** - Creating open communication channels within teams, such as regular team meetings or suggestion boxes, can encourage team members to provide informal feedback on leadership effectiveness.

Chapter 2: Vision and Goals

Strategies for Developing a Clear Vision of Your Desired Leadership Identity

With a wealth of feedback at their disposal and a deeper understanding of their leadership identity, Alex set their sights on the next horizon: crafting a clear and compelling vision for their leadership future. This wasn't just about setting targets for their career but about envisioning the kind of leader they aspired to be and the impact they wished to have on InnovateTech and the broader industry.

Alex began this phase with introspection, dedicating time to meditate and journal about their aspirations. They reflected on leaders they admired, both within and outside the tech industry. These role models ranged from innovative founders of tech giants to transformative figures in social movements. Alex studied their paths, identifying traits that resonated with their own values and leadership style. They were inspired by these leaders' courage, vision, and unwavering commitment to their goals, aiming to embody these traits in their own journey.

Defining their leadership principles became Alex's next step. They distilled their core values into actionable leadership principles, such as fostering innovation, promoting diversity and inclusion, and leading with empathy. These principles would serve as Alex's compass, guiding their decisions and actions.

Visualizing their future self was a powerful exercise. Alex imagined the achievements they wanted to be known for, such as leading InnovateTech to develop groundbreaking technologies that addressed societal challenges, creating an inclusive culture that nurtured talent from all backgrounds, and being a mentor who helped others realize their potential. This vision was not just a dream but a call to action, inspiring Alex to set specific, measurable, achievable, relevant, and time-bound (SMART) goals.

Developing an action plan to achieve these goals involved identifying the skills and knowledge they needed to acquire or strengthen. Alex committed to seeking feedback and mentorship, engaging more deeply with their mentor and expanding their network to include leaders who could offer diverse perspectives and guidance.

Investing in leadership courses became a priority. Alex enrolled in executive leadership programs and workshops on innovation management and diversity and inclusion, seeking to broaden their understanding and apply new insights to their role.

Maintaining a reflective journal became even more critical during this phase. It allowed Alex to track their progress, reflect on their experiences, and adjust their strategies as needed. This practice kept their leadership vision dynamic, adapting to new challenges and opportunities.

This systematic approach to crafting and pursuing their leadership vision enabled Alex to develop a nuanced understanding of the leader they aspired to be. It served as a guiding light for making strategic decisions aligned with their leadership goals and values, ensuring that every step they took was a step toward that envisioned future.

Through this journey, Alex not only transformed their leadership brand but also positioned themselves as a visionary leader within InnovateTech. Their clear vision, grounded in strong values and principles, inspired their team and colleagues, driving innovation and fostering a culture of inclusivity and continuous learning. Alex's leadership vision became a catalyst for their own growth and the advancement of their organization, embodying the true essence of transformative leadership.

Crafting a clear vision for your leadership involves introspection, looking up to inspirational leaders, defining your leadership principles, envisioning your future achievements, setting specific goals, seeking feedback and mentorship, and committing to continuous learning and reflection. By identifying role models and adapting their traits to fit your values, clarifying and articulating your core values as leadership principles, and visualizing your future self, you lay the groundwork for your leadership vision. Setting SMART goals and developing action plans help in achieving this vision, while feedback from peers and guidance from mentors refine it. Investing in leadership courses and maintaining a reflective journal further deepens your understanding of your leadership style and growth areas. This systematic approach enables you to develop a nuanced vision of the leader you aspire to be, serving as a guide for making strategic decisions aligned with your leadership goals and values.

1. Reflect on Inspirational Leaders

- **Identify Role Models**: Think of leaders you admire, both within your industry and from other spheres of life. Note the qualities, behaviors, and values that make them stand out to you.
- **Adapt and Personalize**: Consider which aspects of their leadership style resonate with your personal values and how you can adapt these traits to suit your unique context.

2. Define Your Leadership Principles

- **Core Values Exercise**: Clarify your core values as they are the foundation of your leadership principles. Your values should guide every decision and action you take as a leader.
- **Develop Leadership Principles**: Based on your values, articulate a set of leadership principles that will guide your behavior and decision-making process. These principles serve as your compass in navigating leadership challenges.

3. Envision Your Future Self

- **Future Self Visualization**: Engage in a visualization exercise where you imagine yourself in the future, having achieved your

leadership goals. Consider what kind of leader you are, how you interact with your team, and what achievements you're most proud of.
- **Write a Future Biography**: Write a brief biography of yourself as a future leader, highlighting your accomplishments, the challenges you've overcome, and the impact you've made.

4. Set Specific Leadership Goals

- **SMART Goals**: Use the SMART criteria (Specific, Measurable, Achievable, Relevant, Time-bound) to set clear and actionable leadership goals. These goals should align with the broader vision you have for your leadership journey.
- **Action Plans**: For each goal, develop an action plan detailing the steps you need to take, resources required, and milestones to track progress.

5. Seek Feedback and Mentorship

- **360-Degree Feedback**: Obtain feedback from peers, subordinates, and superiors on your current leadership style and areas for improvement. This holistic view can provide insights into how you're perceived and where you can grow.
- **Find a Mentor**: Seek out a mentor who embodies the type of leader you aspire to become. A mentor can provide guidance, advice, and feedback to help you refine your vision and approach.

6. Continuous Learning and Reflection

- **Leadership Courses and Reading**: Invest in leadership development courses, workshops, and books. Learning from experts and thought leaders can inspire new ideas and strategies for personal growth.
- **Reflective Journaling**: Maintain a leadership journal where you regularly reflect on your experiences, challenges faced, and lessons learned. This practice can deepen your understanding of your leadership style and growth areas.

By systematically working through these techniques, you can develop a nuanced and compelling vision of the leader you aspire to become. This vision will serve as a guidepost for your development efforts, helping you to make strategic choices that align with your leadership goals and values.

Fill in the Blank Questions

1. Reflecting on _____ leaders can help define and refine your leadership vision by identifying qualities and values that resonate with you.
2. Setting _____ goals involves using criteria that ensure goals are specific, measurable, achievable, relevant, and time-bound.
3. Seeking _____ from peers, subordinates, and superiors provides a holistic view of your current leadership style and areas for improvement.
4. Continuous learning and _____ help deepen your understanding of your leadership style and growth areas.

Multiple Choice Questions

1. **Which exercise helps in identifying the foundation of your leadership principles?** A) Core Values Exercise B) Future Self Visualization C) 360-Degree Feedback D) Reflective Journaling
2. **What is the purpose of setting SMART goals in leadership development?** A) To ensure goals are vague and flexible B) To make goals specific, measurable, achievable, relevant, and time-bound C) To reduce the importance of goal setting D) To focus solely on short-term objectives
3. **How can feedback and mentorship contribute to leadership development?** A) By limiting a leader's perspective B) By providing insights into leadership style and areas for improvement C) By discouraging new strategies and ideas D) By focusing only on past achievements
4. **What role does continuous learning play in crafting a leadership vision?** A) It discourages adaptation and growth B) It minimizes the need for reflection C) It inspires new ideas and strategies for personal growth D) It focuses solely on reinforcing existing skills

Books:

1. **"The Leadership Challenge: How to Make Extraordinary Things Happen in Organizations"** by James M. Kouzes and Barry Z. Posner - This book outlines a practical framework for developing a clear vision and effective leadership skills based on extensive research and real-world examples.
2. **"Dare to Lead: Brave Work. Tough Conversations. Whole Hearts."** by Brené Brown - Brené Brown offers insights into crafting a vision for leadership that is rooted in courage, vulnerability, and authenticity, emphasizing the importance of aligning values with actions.
3. **"Start with Why: How Great Leaders Inspire Everyone to Take Action"** by Simon Sinek - Simon Sinek explores the concept of starting with a clear "why" as the foundation for leadership vision, inspiring others to follow and commit to shared goals.

Additional Resources:

1. **Leadership Workshops and Seminars** - Participating in workshops and seminars focused on leadership development, offered by organizations, universities, or professional associations, provides opportunities to refine your vision and learn from experts and peers.
2. **Mentorship Programs** - Engaging with mentors who have experience in leadership roles can provide valuable guidance and feedback as you craft and refine your leadership vision. Many organizations offer formal mentorship programs, or you can seek out individual mentors in your network.
3. **Online Visioning Tools** - Websites like MindTools offer interactive tools and resources for developing a personal leadership vision, setting goals, and creating action plans to achieve them.
4. **Reflective Practices** - Incorporating daily or weekly reflection into your routine, through journaling or meditation, allows you to deepen your understanding of your leadership vision and track your progress towards your goals over time.

5. **Leadership Assessment Tools** - Online platforms like Center for Creative Leadership and Hogan Assessments offer assessments and tools to help leaders gain insights into their leadership styles, strengths, and areas for development, which can inform the crafting of their leadership vision.

Aligning Personal and Professional Aspirations: Establishing Short-Term and Long-Term Leadership Goals

With the vision for their leadership firmly in place, Alex turned their focus to setting tangible goals that would bridge the gap between their current reality and their envisioned future. They understood that achieving their ultimate vision of transformative leadership at InnovateTech and beyond required a strategic blend of short-term and long-term goals. This approach would not only focus their efforts but also ensure a structured path for their development and impact.

Alex started with short-term goals, which they defined as objectives to be achieved within the next 1 to 12 months. These goals were practical and immediate, aimed at enhancing their capabilities and leadership effectiveness in the near term. One of Alex's primary short-term goals was to improve their communication skills, especially in conveying complex ideas clearly and inspiring their team. They planned to achieve this through workshops and by seeking regular feedback from their peers and mentors.

Another goal was to develop specific leadership abilities, such as emotional intelligence and conflict resolution. Alex recognized these skills were crucial for leading a diverse and innovative team effectively. They committed to a mentorship program, both as a mentor and a mentee, to learn from the experiences of others and to share their own.

Expanding their professional network was also a key short-term goal. Alex aimed to connect with leaders and innovators across the tech industry, understanding that these relationships would be invaluable for personal growth and for fostering partnerships that could benefit InnovateTech.

Finally, leading a high-stakes project successfully was a significant short-term goal. Alex wanted to demonstrate their capability to manage complex challenges, deliver exceptional results, and inspire their team to exceed expectations.

For the long-term, stretching over 1 to 5 years, Alex's goals were more strategic and aligned with the leader they aspired to become. One such goal was to attain a senior leadership position within InnovateTech, where they could have a broader impact on the company's direction and innovation strategy.

Mentoring others became a passionate long-term aspiration for Alex. They envisioned creating a leadership development program within InnovateTech to nurture emerging leaders, sharing their experiences and insights to help others grow.

Building high-performing teams was another long-term goal. Alex planned to leverage their skills and network to attract top talent and foster a culture of excellence, innovation, and inclusivity.

Leading organizational change was perhaps Alex's most ambitious long-term goal. They aimed to spearhead initiatives that would not only drive technological innovation but also ensure that InnovateTech was a leader in corporate social responsibility within the tech industry.

Achieving these goals required Alex to employ a systematic approach, characterized by clarity, measurability, actionable plans, accountability, and the flexibility to adapt based on feedback and changing circumstances. Alex set clear milestones for each goal and developed detailed action plans outlining the steps needed to achieve them. They sought accountability through regular check-ins with their mentor and feedback sessions with their team.

As Alex embarked on this journey of achieving their short-term and long-term goals, they remained open to learning and adapting their plans based on new insights and feedback. This structured yet flexible approach ensured that Alex was not only progressing towards their leadership vision but also contributing significantly to InnovateTech's success and inspiring others along the way.

This journey of setting and pursuing strategic goals demonstrated Alex's commitment to continuous growth and development as a leader. It was a testament to the power of visionary leadership, grounded in clear goals and driven by a dedication to making a lasting impact.

Setting short-term and long-term leadership goals is essential for personal and professional development, guiding leaders toward their ultimate vision. Short-term goals, ranging from 1 to 12 months, are focused on immediate improvements such as enhancing communication skills, developing specific leadership abilities, expanding professional networks, and leading projects successfully. These goals lay the foundation for achieving long-term aspirations over 1 to 5 years, which are more strategic and aligned with becoming the leader one aims to be, including attaining leadership positions, mentoring others, building high-performing teams, and leading organizational change. Achieving these goals requires clarity, measurability, actionable plans, accountability, and the flexibility to adjust based on feedback and changing circumstances. This systematic approach to goal setting not only focuses efforts and measures progress but also serves as a roadmap for continuous leadership growth and development.

Short-term Leadership Goals (1-12 months)

Short-term goals focus on immediate improvements and achievements that lay the groundwork for your long-term vision.

Examples and Strategies:

1. **Enhance Communication Skills**: Aim to improve your clarity, empathy, and effectiveness in communication. This could

involve taking a course on communication, seeking feedback from peers, or practicing public speaking.
2. **Develop a Specific Leadership Skill**: Identify a leadership skill you want to develop, such as conflict resolution, time management, or emotional intelligence. Set a goal to attend workshops or training sessions and apply these skills in your daily interactions.
3. **Expand Your Professional Network**: Aim to connect with a certain number of professionals within and outside your industry. Attend networking events, join professional organizations, and actively participate in industry forums.
4. **Lead a Project Successfully**: Volunteer to lead a new project or initiative in your organization. This provides a tangible opportunity to apply your leadership skills and make a direct impact.

Long-term Leadership Goals (1-5 years)

Long-term goals are more strategic and align with your ultimate vision of the leader you want to become. They often require ongoing effort and dedication.

Examples and Strategies:

1. **Achieve a Leadership Position**: Target a specific leadership role within your organization or industry. Develop a career path strategy, including necessary qualifications, experiences, and milestones to achieve this position.
2. **Mentor and Develop Others**: Aim to mentor a certain number of emerging leaders or contribute to the development programs within your organization. This goal reinforces your role as a leader who invests in the growth of others.
3. **Build a High-Performing Team**: Focus on creating a team known for its excellence, innovation, and collaborative culture. This involves long-term investment in team development, culture building, and talent management.
4. **Influence Organizational Change**: Set a goal to lead a significant change initiative, such as implementing a new

technology, restructuring a department, or fostering a more inclusive workplace culture.

Setting and Achieving Your Goals

- **Specificity and Measurability**: Clearly define what success looks like for each goal. Use specific metrics or milestones to measure progress.
- **Action Plans**: For each goal, draft an action plan detailing the steps you'll take, resources needed, and a timeline for achievement.
- **Accountability**: Share your goals with a mentor, coach, or peer group who can provide support, feedback, and hold you accountable.
- **Review and Adjust**: Regularly review your goals and progress. Be prepared to adjust your plans based on feedback and changing circumstances.

Setting well-defined short-term and long-term goals is a dynamic process that helps you focus your efforts, measure progress, and achieve the leadership success you aspire to. Remember, the journey of leadership is continuous, and these goals serve as milestones that guide your growth and development.

Fill in the Blank Questions

1. Short-term leadership goals focus on immediate improvements and are typically set for a period of ___ to ___ months.
2. Developing a specific leadership skill, such as _____ resolution or time management, is an example of a short-term goal.
3. Long-term goals often require ongoing effort and are aligned with the ultimate vision of the leader you want to become, usually set for ___ to ___ years.
4. To achieve leadership goals, it's important to draft an _____ plan detailing the steps you'll take and resources needed.

Multiple Choice Questions

1. **Which of the following is NOT typically considered a short-term leadership goal?** A) Enhancing communication skills B) Achieving a leadership position C) Expanding your professional network D) Leading a project successfully
2. **What is crucial for setting and achieving leadership goals?** A) Ignoring feedback B) Lack of clarity C) Specificity and measurability D) Avoiding accountability
3. **Long-term leadership goals may include:** A) Taking a short course B) Attending a single networking event C) Influencing organizational change D) Improving a skill overnight
4. **An action plan for achieving leadership goals should NOT include:** A) Resources needed B) A timeline for achievement C) Reasons to avoid feedback D) Steps you'll take

Books:

1. **"The 7 Habits of Highly Effective People: Powerful Lessons in Personal Change"** by Stephen R. Covey - This classic book offers insights into effective goal setting, prioritization, and personal development, providing a framework for setting both short-term and long-term goals aligned with one's values and vision.
2. **"Drive: The Surprising Truth About What Motivates Us"** by Daniel H. Pink - Daniel Pink explores the science of motivation and goal setting, offering practical strategies for setting goals that inspire and drive performance, essential for leadership development.
3. **"Measure What Matters: Online Tools for Understanding Customers, Social Media, Engagement, and Key Relationships"** by John Doerr - John Doerr introduces the concept of Objectives and Key Results (OKRs), a goal-setting framework widely used by organizations like Google and Intel, which can be adapted for personal and leadership goal setting.

Additional Resources:

1. **Leadership Development Programs** - Many organizations offer leadership development programs that include goal-setting workshops, coaching sessions, and resources to help leaders set and achieve their short-term and long-term goals.
2. **Online Goal-Setting Tools** - Websites like GoalsOnTrack and Todoist offer digital platforms for setting, tracking, and managing both short-term and long-term goals, providing reminders and progress tracking features to keep leaders accountable.
3. **Professional Networking Events** - Attending networking events, conferences, and seminars in your industry or field allows leaders to expand their professional networks and gain insights from peers and experts, supporting the achievement of both short-term and long-term leadership goals.
4. **Leadership Coaching** - Working with a leadership coach can provide personalized guidance and support in setting and achieving goals, helping leaders overcome obstacles and stay focused on their development objectives.
5. **Leadership Development Books and Articles** - Continuously reading books, articles, and blogs on leadership development provides leaders with insights, strategies, and inspiration for setting and achieving their goals, staying updated on best practices and trends in leadership.

Chapter 3: Crafting Your Leadership Brand Statement

Crafting Your Distinctive Leadership Brand Statement: A Step-by-Step Guide

With their goals mapped out and a clear path forward, Alex next focused on crystallizing their leadership identity through a leadership brand statement. This was not just about summarizing their professional persona but about capturing the essence of their leadership in a way that was both authentic and compelling. Alex understood that this statement would serve as their north star, guiding their actions and decisions, and communicating their leadership brand to the world.

The process began with deep reflection. Alex revisited their core values, reaffirming that integrity, empathy, innovation, and inclusivity were the pillars of their leadership. They considered the feedback they had received and the strengths that had been highlighted, such as strategic vision, emotional intelligence, and the ability to inspire and drive change.

Clarifying their leadership vision was the next step. Alex envisioned the impact they wanted to have: leading their team and InnovateTech towards groundbreaking innovation while fostering a culture that valued diversity and continuous learning. They imagined the legacy they wished to leave behind—a legacy of mentorship, empowerment, and transformation.

With these elements in mind, Alex began drafting their leadership brand statement. They aimed to weave together their values, strengths, and vision into a coherent narrative. After several iterations, they crafted a statement that felt true to their identity:

"I lead with integrity and empathy, driving innovation and inclusivity to empower my team and shape the future of technology.

My vision is to inspire and mentor the next generation of leaders, leaving a legacy of transformative impact."

This statement was concise yet powerful, encapsulating Alex's leadership essence and aspirations.

Before finalizing their leadership brand statement, Alex sought feedback from trusted colleagues and their mentor. This feedback was invaluable, providing perspectives that helped refine the statement, making it more impactful and aligned with how others perceived Alex's leadership.

With their leadership brand statement finalized, Alex began to live out this identity more intentionally. They used the statement to guide their daily actions and decisions, ensuring consistency between their brand and their behavior. Alex also integrated their leadership brand statement into their professional profile, including social media platforms and their biography on the InnovateTech website, communicating their leadership essence to a broader audience.

As their career progressed, Alex remained mindful that their leadership brand statement was not static. They revisited and reflected on their statement regularly, recognizing that as they grew and the world around them changed, their leadership brand would also evolve. This ongoing process of reflection and adjustment ensured that Alex's leadership brand remained relevant and authentic, truly reflecting who they were as a leader and the impact they aimed to achieve.

Through this meticulous process of crafting, refining, and living their leadership brand statement, Alex not only solidified their identity as a leader but also inspired those around them. Their leadership brand became a beacon, guiding their path forward, influencing their interactions, and shaping their legacy. It was a testament to the power of a clear, coherent leadership identity, rooted in core values and vision, and expressed with conviction and authenticity.

Creating a concise and impactful leadership brand statement is a reflective process that synthesizes your core values, strengths, and vision into a coherent identity. Beginning with identifying and prioritizing your essential values such as integrity and empathy, you move on to acknowledging your strengths through self-assessment tools and feedback. Clarifying your leadership vision involves envisioning the impact and legacy you aim to leave behind. Drafting your leadership brand statement then entails combining these elements into a clear, concise narrative, refined with feedback from trusted colleagues, and finalized into a statement that embodies your leadership essence. This statement, a vivid articulation of who you are as a leader, guides your actions and decisions, ensuring they align with your values and vision. Living your leadership brand means consistently demonstrating these values and strengths, using your statement to communicate your brand across professional platforms. As your career progresses, your leadership brand statement will evolve, necessitating regular reflection and adjustment to remain relevant and authentic.

Step 1: Reflect on Your Core Values

- **Identify Your Values**: List the values that are most important to you in your leadership role. These might include integrity, innovation, respect, empathy, or accountability.
- **Prioritize**: Narrow down your list to the top three to five values that are non-negotiable in your leadership practice.

Step 2: Acknowledge Your Strengths

- **Self-Assessment**: Use tools such as the StrengthsFinder or solicit feedback from peers and subordinates to identify your key strengths.
- **Select Relevant Strengths**: Choose strengths that align with your leadership values and vision, and that you consistently leverage to achieve your goals.

Step 3: Clarify Your Leadership Vision

- **Envision Your Impact**: Think about the legacy you want to leave and the impact you wish to have through your leadership.
- **Articulate Your Vision**: Write a sentence or two that encapsulates your vision for your leadership journey.

Step 4: Draft Your Leadership Brand Statement

- **Combine Elements**: Start by drafting sentences that combine your core values, strengths, and leadership vision. Don't worry about length or clarity at this stage; focus on getting your ideas down.
- **Refine and Simplify**: Review your draft and start to refine it. Aim for a statement that is no more than two to three sentences long. It should clearly and concisely convey who you are as a leader, what you stand for, and the impact you aim to have.

Step 5: Seek Feedback

- **Consult with Trusted Colleagues**: Share your draft statement with mentors, peers, or trusted colleagues to get their input. Ask if it resonates and reflects the leader they see in you.
- **Revise Accordingly**: Use the feedback to make revisions. This might involve clarifying your message, adjusting your language, or further simplifying your statement.

Step 6: Finalize Your Statement

- **Polish Your Statement**: Make any final tweaks to your statement to ensure it is impactful and reflects your authentic leadership brand.
- **Commit to It**: Once finalized, commit your leadership brand statement to memory. It should guide your actions, decisions, and how you present yourself to others.

Step 7: Live Your Leadership Brand

- **Align Actions with Your Statement**: Consistently demonstrate the values, strengths, and vision outlined in your leadership brand statement in your daily actions and decisions.
- **Communicate Your Brand**: Use your leadership brand statement in your professional bio, LinkedIn profile, and in conversations about your leadership style and goals.

Example of a Leadership Brand Statement

"I lead with empathy, integrity, and a commitment to excellence, leveraging my strengths in strategic thinking and communication to inspire my team to achieve innovative solutions and make a meaningful impact."

Remember, your leadership brand statement is a living part of your professional identity. It may evolve as you grow and take on new challenges in your leadership journey. Regular reflection and adjustment will ensure it remains aligned with your values, strengths, and vision.

Fill in the Blank Questions

1. Identifying and prioritizing your core values is the first step in creating a _____ leadership brand statement.
2. Using tools like StrengthsFinder helps in acknowledging your key _____ that align with your leadership brand.
3. Envisioning the _____ you want to leave helps clarify your leadership vision.
4. Your leadership brand statement should be refined with feedback from _____ colleagues.

Multiple Choice Questions

1. **What is the purpose of identifying core values in the process of creating a leadership brand statement?** A) To increase

financial profit B) To clarify personal and professional goals C) To decide on office decor D) To simplify daily routines
2. **How can strengths be identified for a leadership brand statement?** A) Guessing based on past successes B) Using self-assessment tools and feedback C) Following the latest trends D) Copying a colleague's strengths
3. **What role does envisioning your legacy play in crafting your leadership vision?** A) Determines your vacation plans B) Guides the choice of office equipment C) Helps clarify the impact you aim to have D) Influences your choice of wardrobe
4. **The final leadership brand statement should be:** A) As long as a novel B) Focused on past achievements only C) Clear, concise, and reflective of your leadership identity D) Written by someone else to ensure objectivity

Books:

1. "**Dare to Lead: Brave Work. Tough Conversations. Whole Hearts**." by Brené Brown - Brené Brown explores the concept of leadership grounded in authenticity, courage, and vulnerability, providing insights and exercises to help leaders define their values and develop their leadership brand statement.
2. "**StrengthsFinder 2.0**" by Tom Rath - This book includes an assessment tool that helps individuals identify their strengths and talents, essential for crafting a leadership brand statement that reflects one's unique abilities and contributions.
3. "**The Leadership Challenge: How to Make Extraordinary Things Happen in Organizations**" by James M. Kouzes and Barry Z. Posner - Kouzes and Posner present a framework for effective leadership development, emphasizing the importance of clarity of values and vision in creating a compelling leadership brand statement.

Additional Resources:

1. **Leadership Branding Workshops** - Many organizations and leadership development programs offer workshops specifically focused on crafting a leadership brand statement, providing

guidance, exercises, and peer feedback to help participants articulate their leadership identity.
2. **Leadership Assessment Tools** - Online platforms like Gallup's CliftonStrengths and VIA Character offer assessments to help individuals identify their core values, strengths, and character traits, serving as valuable resources for shaping a leadership brand statement.
3. **Executive Coaching** - Working with an executive coach can provide personalized support and guidance in clarifying values, strengths, and vision, as well as crafting and refining a leadership brand statement tailored to individual leadership goals and aspirations.
4. **Peer Feedback Groups** - Joining or forming peer feedback groups allows leaders to receive input and perspectives from trusted colleagues, helping them refine their leadership brand statement through constructive feedback and diverse insights.
5. **Online Articles and Templates** - Various articles and resources are available online that provide guidance and templates for crafting a leadership brand statement, offering step-by-step instructions and examples to assist leaders in articulating their leadership identity effectively.

Effective Examples of Leadership Brand Statements: Inspiring Models for Professional Identity

As Alex integrated their leadership brand statement into their daily life and professional identity, they found it to be a beacon, guiding their decisions and interactions. It was a declaration of their commitment not just to the goals and achievements they sought but to the kind of leader they aspired to be—innovative, empathetic, integrity-driven, strategic, empowering, collaborative, and inclusive.

Drawing on the broad spectrum of leadership philosophies that inspired them—from innovation-driven leadership that breaks new ground, to empathetic leadership that nurtures growth, to servant leadership that elevates others—Alex's statement was a mirror to their multifaceted leadership style. It was not just a reflection of their current identity but a vision of the leader they were continually striving to become. This dynamic approach allowed Alex to remain adaptable, embracing the fluidity of leadership in the face of evolving challenges and opportunities.

In living out their leadership brand, Alex found new ways to embody these principles. Fostering innovation became not just about leading projects but about creating a culture where creativity and risk-taking were encouraged, where failure was seen as a steppingstone to success. Prioritizing empathy meant truly listening to their team, understanding their perspectives, and supporting their growth and well-being. Upholding integrity involved making tough decisions that stayed true to their values, even when faced with pressure to compromise.

Envisioning strategic goals was about looking beyond the immediate, charting a course for InnovateTech that anticipated future trends and challenges. Empowering others became a daily practice, where Alex sought to delegate meaningful responsibilities, providing the guidance and trust needed for their team to excel. Championing collaboration and inclusivity meant breaking down silos, encouraging diverse voices and ideas, and creating a sense of belonging and purpose.

As Alex's leadership journey unfolded, their brand statement served as a touchstone, reminding them of the leader they aimed to be. It influenced how they led meetings, how they interacted with colleagues, how they approached problem-solving, and how they made strategic decisions. It was evident in their communication, their policies, and the initiatives they championed.

Moreover, Alex's leadership brand became a source of inspiration within InnovateTech. It attracted like-minded professionals to their team, fostered a loyal and highly motivated group of followers, and set a standard for leadership within the organization. Others began to look to Alex not just for direction in projects but for guidance in their personal leadership journeys, seeing Alex's approach as a model to aspire to.

This ripple effect extended beyond InnovateTech. Alex's commitment to their leadership brand statement, coupled with their achievements and the culture they fostered, garnered attention in the wider tech community. They were invited to speak at conferences, contribute to industry publications, and participate in leadership forums, where they shared their insights and experiences, encouraging others to craft and live by their leadership brand statements.

> Through this journey, Alex discovered that a leadership brand statement is much more than words on a page. It is a living, breathing embodiment of one's leadership identity. It requires not just the initial reflection and articulation but a commitment to embodying its principles every day. As Alex's story illustrates, the power of a clear, authentic leadership brand statement lies not just in guiding the individual leader but in inspiring those around them, shaping a legacy of leadership that transcends individual achievements to influence the broader community.

Crafting a personal leadership brand statement involves distilling your unique leadership approach, core values, and desired impact into a succinct and compelling declaration. Drawing inspiration from examples like innovation-driven leadership, empathetic leadership for growth, integrity-based decision making, strategic visionary outlook, servant leadership for empowerment, and collaborative and inclusive leadership, you can articulate your own leadership brand statement. Whether it's fostering innovation, prioritizing empathy, upholding integrity, envisioning strategic goals, empowering others, or championing collaboration and inclusivity, your statement should reflect your authentic leadership essence and guide your leadership journey.

1. **Innovation-Driven Leadership**: "I harness the power of innovation to transform challenges into opportunities, fostering a culture where creativity leads the way to groundbreaking solutions."
2. **Empathetic Leadership for Growth**: "Through empathy and understanding, I build strong, resilient teams poised for growth,

ensuring each member feels valued, heard, and motivated to excel."
3. **Integrity-Based Decision Making**: "Guided by unwavering integrity, I make decisions that reflect our collective values, leading by example to inspire trust and authenticity within my team."
4. **Strategic Visionary**: "With a strategic approach and a visionary outlook, I steer our team towards achieving long-term success, embracing change and leveraging opportunities for continuous improvement."
5. **Servant Leadership for Empowerment**: "As a servant leader, I prioritize the development and well-being of my team, empowering them to achieve their full potential while collectively advancing our mission."
6. **Collaborative and Inclusive Leadership**: "I champion collaboration and inclusivity, creating an environment where diverse perspectives are celebrated, and every team member can contribute to our shared success."

Remember, a leadership brand statement should reflect your unique approach to leadership, your core values, and the impact you aim to have. It's about encapsulating your leadership essence in a concise and compelling way that resonates with others and guides your actions and decisions.

Fill in the Blank Questions

1. "I harness the power of innovation to transform challenges into _____."
2. "Through empathy and understanding, I build strong, resilient teams poised for _____."
3. "Guided by unwavering integrity, I make decisions that reflect our collective _____."
4. "With a strategic approach and a visionary outlook, I steer our team towards achieving _____ success."

Multiple Choice Questions

1. **What is emphasized in the leadership brand statement, "Empathetic Leadership for Growth"?** A) Decisiveness B) Growth and resilience of teams C) Innovation D) Technical skills
2. **What is highlighted in the leadership brand statement, "Servant Leadership for Empowerment"?** A) Prioritizing personal goals B) Empowering team members C) Individual achievement D) Centralized decision-making
3. **Which aspect is central to the leadership brand statement, "Collaborative and Inclusive Leadership"?** A) Micro-management B) Celebrating diverse perspectives C) Autocratic leadership D) Individual competition
4. **What is the purpose of these illustrative examples in crafting a personal leadership brand statement?** A) To copy directly B) To limit creativity C) To inspire and guide the creation of one's unique statement D) To discourage personal reflection

Books:

1. "**Leaders Eat Last: Why Some Teams Pull Together and Others Don't**" by Simon Sinek - Sinek explores the concept of servant leadership and its impact on team dynamics, providing insights into crafting a leadership brand statement centered around empowerment and collaboration.
2. "**The Innovator's DNA: Mastering the Five Skills of Disruptive Innovators**" by Jeff Dyer, Hal Gregersen, and Clayton M. Christensen - This book delves into the traits and behaviors of innovative leaders, offering inspiration and guidance for crafting a leadership brand statement focused on fostering innovation and visionary thinking.
3. "**Daring Greatly: How the Courage to Be Vulnerable Transforms the Way We Live, Love, Parent, and Lead**" by Brené Brown - Brown's exploration of vulnerability and courage in leadership can inspire leaders to incorporate empathy and authenticity into their leadership brand statement, prioritizing growth and connection.

Additional Resources:

1. **Leadership Branding Workshops** - Participating in workshops focused on leadership branding can provide practical exercises and guidance for crafting a personal leadership brand statement, drawing from various leadership styles and examples for inspiration.
2. **Mentorship and Coaching** - Seeking mentorship or coaching from experienced leaders can offer personalized support and feedback in refining and articulating a leadership brand statement aligned with individual values and goals.
3. **TED Talks and Podcasts** - TED Talks and podcasts featuring leadership experts and thought leaders offer valuable insights and examples of different leadership styles, providing inspiration and ideas for crafting a compelling leadership brand statement.
4. **Online Articles and Templates** - Various online articles and resources provide templates and frameworks for crafting a personal leadership brand statement, offering step-by-step guidance and examples to help leaders articulate their unique leadership essence effectively.

Chapter 4: Communicating Your Leadership Brand

Strategies for Strategic Communication: Effectively Transmitting Your Leadership Brand Across Multiple Channels

Alex took the task of communicating their leadership brand seriously, understanding that consistency across various channels was crucial for reinforcing their identity and ensuring they were perceived as intended. They knew that each platform and interaction offered a unique opportunity to showcase their leadership essence and connect with different audiences.

On social media, Alex carefully tailored their content to reflect their leadership values and vision. They shared insights on innovation, posted articles on empathy and inclusivity in the workplace, and celebrated team successes, ensuring each post resonated with their brand of empowering and visionary leadership. LinkedIn became a vital tool for Alex, where they meticulously curated their profile to mirror their leadership brand statement. They shared thought leadership pieces, engaged with content from other leaders, and participated in discussions that underscored their commitment to innovation and collaborative leadership.

Networking events and professional associations offered Alex a stage to embody their leadership brand in real-time interactions. They approached these opportunities with intention, engaging thoughtfully in conversations, offering insights that reflected their values, and connecting with individuals in a manner that underscored their approachable and inclusive leadership style.

But for Alex, effectively communicating their leadership brand went beyond digital platforms and public events; it was about maintaining consistency in personal interactions as well. Whether it was a team meeting, a one-on-one with a colleague, or an impromptu chat by the coffee machine, Alex ensured their behavior and decisions consistently reflected their leadership principles. This commitment to authenticity in every interaction reinforced their brand identity among their peers and team members.

To establish themselves as a thought leader in their field, Alex leveraged opportunities to publish articles in industry publications and speak at conferences. These platforms allowed them to share their insights on leading edge technology and organizational culture, further solidifying their reputation as an innovative and empathetic leader.

Understanding the importance of digital presence, Alex also optimized their online profiles and content for searchability, ensuring that those looking for insights in their areas of expertise could easily find their work. This strategic approach helped expand their influence beyond their immediate network, reaching a global audience.

A consistent visual identity across all platforms and communications further reinforced Alex's leadership brand. They chose imagery and design elements that reflected the innovative and inclusive nature of their leadership, ensuring a cohesive and recognizable brand presence online and offline.

By employing these strategies, Alex not only effectively communicated their leadership brand but also established themselves as a respected thought leader in the tech industry. Their consistent and authentic brand presence garnered respect from peers and industry professionals alike, attracting opportunities for collaboration, mentorship, and leadership that aligned with their vision and values. Through deliberate and strategic communication, Alex demonstrated that a well-articulated and consistently presented leadership brand could indeed open doors, influence change, and leave a lasting impact.

Effectively communicating your leadership brand across various channels is essential for reinforcing your leadership identity and ensuring consistency in how you're perceived by others. Strategies tailored for different platforms include tailoring content on social media to align with your brand, ensuring professional profiles reflect your brand on platforms like LinkedIn, engaging thoughtfully in networking events and associations to showcase your brand, maintaining consistent behavior in personal interactions, publishing articles and speaking at events to establish thought leadership, optimizing digital presence for searchability, and maintaining a consistent visual identity across platforms. By employing these strategies, you can effectively communicate and reinforce your leadership brand, establishing yourself as a thought leader in your field and gaining respect from your peers and industry.

1. Social Media

- **Tailor Your Content**: Align your posts, comments, and shares with your leadership brand. For example, if your brand emphasizes innovation, share and comment on the latest industry trends or technologies.
- **Professional Profile**: Ensure your LinkedIn profile reflects your leadership brand. This includes a professional photo, a compelling summary that incorporates your leadership brand statement, and highlights of your accomplishments that align with your brand.
- **Engage Thoughtfully**: Engage with your network by commenting on and sharing relevant content. Thoughtful engagement can position you as a thoughtful leader in your field.

2. Professional Networks

- **Networking Events**: Attend industry networking events, conferences, and seminars. Prepare an elevator pitch that succinctly conveys your leadership brand, allowing you to introduce yourself effectively.
- **Professional Associations**: Join and actively participate in professional associations related to your field. Volunteer for

leadership roles in these organizations to demonstrate your leadership qualities and commitment.
- **Mentorship**: Offer mentorship to others in your industry. This not only helps you solidify your leadership brand but also allows you to give back and support the growth of emerging leaders.

3. Personal Interactions

- **Consistent Behavior**: Ensure that your interactions with colleagues, subordinates, and superiors reflect your leadership brand. Consistency in behavior, from formal meetings to casual conversations, reinforces your brand.
- **Feedback Solicitation**: Regularly ask for feedback on your leadership style and approach. Use this feedback to refine how you communicate your leadership brand in interpersonal interactions.
- **Storytelling**: Use storytelling in your communications to share experiences, lessons learned, and success stories that highlight your leadership qualities and vision.

4. Thought Leadership

- **Publish Articles**: Write articles or blog posts on topics relevant to your leadership brand and industry expertise. Share these on LinkedIn, industry forums, or personal blogs.
- **Speak at Events**: Seek opportunities to speak at industry events, webinars, or podcasts. Public speaking allows you to articulate your leadership vision and values to a broader audience.

5. Digital Presence

- **Personal Website**: Consider creating a personal website or portfolio that showcases your achievements, projects, and thought leadership articles. This can serve as a central hub for your professional brand.
- **SEO for Your Name**: Optimize your online content with your name and relevant keywords to ensure that searches for your name bring up content that reinforces your leadership brand.

6. Visual Branding

- **Consistent Visual Identity**: Use a consistent visual identity across all platforms, including a professional portrait and any branding elements like logos or color schemes, to make your leadership brand instantly recognizable.

By strategically utilizing these channels, you can effectively communicate and reinforce your leadership brand, ensuring that your professional identity is clearly understood and respected by your peers, subordinates, and industry at large.

Fill in the Blank Questions

1. When using social media to communicate your leadership brand, ensure your posts, comments, and shares are aligned with your _____.
2. Attend industry networking events and conferences to introduce yourself effectively with an _____ pitch that conveys your leadership brand.
3. Regularly ask for feedback on your leadership style and approach to refine how you communicate your leadership brand in _____ interactions.

Multiple Choice Questions

1. **What is one strategy mentioned for effectively communicating your leadership brand on social media?** A) Randomly sharing any industry-related content B) Engaging with irrelevant content to widen your network C) Tailoring content to align with your leadership brand D) Avoiding engagement with your network
2. **How can attending professional networking events contribute to communicating your leadership brand?** A) By avoiding such events to maintain exclusivity B) By showcasing your disinterest in industry developments C) By effectively introducing yourself with a pitch that conveys your leadership

brand D) By refraining from participating in any networking activities
3. **What is the importance of consistent behavior in personal interactions when communicating your leadership brand?** A) It's unnecessary and may hinder professional relationships B) It helps reinforce your brand and build trust C) It's solely for the purpose of impressing superiors D) It's irrelevant as long as formal meetings are conducted appropriately

Books:

1. "**Building Your Brand: A Practical Guide for School Leaders**" by Joe Sanfelippo and Tony Sinanis - This book offers insights and strategies specifically tailored for educational leaders to effectively communicate their brand and establish themselves as influential leaders in the education sector.
2. "**Leadership Brand: Developing Customer-Focused Leaders to Drive Performance and Build Lasting Value**" by Dave Ulrich and Norm Smallwood - Ulrich and Smallwood provide a comprehensive guide to building and communicating a leadership brand that focuses on driving organizational performance and creating lasting value.
3. "**Brand Identity Breakthrough: How to Craft Your Company's Unique Story to Make Your Products Irresistible**" by Gregory V. Diehl - Although primarily focused on branding for businesses, this book offers valuable principles and strategies for crafting a compelling personal brand story that resonates with your audience and effectively communicates your leadership identity.

Additional Resources:

1. **Online Branding Courses** - Platforms like Udemy, Coursera, and LinkedIn Learning offer courses specifically focused on personal branding and effective communication strategies, providing practical skills and techniques for enhancing your leadership brand across various channels.
2. **Executive Presence Workshops** - Participating in executive presence workshops can help leaders refine their communication

skills, develop a compelling personal brand narrative, and effectively convey their leadership identity in professional settings and interactions.
3. **Networking and Public Speaking Events** - Actively engaging in networking events and opportunities to speak at conferences or industry gatherings allows leaders to showcase their leadership brand through personal interactions and thought leadership presentations, enhancing their visibility and influence within their professional communities.
4. **Social Media Branding Guides** - Various online resources and guides provide tips and best practices for leveraging social media platforms to effectively communicate and reinforce your leadership brand, ensuring consistency and relevance in your online presence.

The Significance of Consistency in Verbal and Non-Verbal Communication: Strengthening Your Leadership Brand

Alex recognized the significance of consistency in both verbal and non-verbal communication for reinforcing their leadership brand. They knew that every interaction was an opportunity to build trust, establish credibility, and showcase their professional identity. To Alex, communication was not just about what they said but how they said it, and perhaps more importantly, how they acted.

In every presentation, meeting, and casual conversation, Alex made sure their verbal communication was clear, articulate, and reflective of their leadership values. They spoke with conviction about innovation, empathized openly with team challenges, and communicated decisions with transparency and integrity. This consistent verbal communication enhanced Alex's influence, making their vision and directives more persuasive to their team and peers.

Non-verbal cues were equally important to Alex. They were mindful of their body language during interactions, ensuring it conveyed openness and confidence. Their facial expressions mirrored genuine interest and empathy during conversations, making others feel valued and understood. Even their professional appearance was chosen thoughtfully to align with their brand, striking a balance between innovation-driven creativity and approachable professionalism.

Alex understood that consistency in these areas was key to building trust. Their team and colleagues knew what to expect from them, not just in terms of what they would say but also how they would react and respond in various situations. This predictability, rooted in a deep alignment with their leadership brand, fostered a strong sense of trust and reliability among those they led.

Credibility came from this alignment as well. When Alex's actions matched their words, it reinforced their authority and expertise. Their consistent communication—both verbal and non-verbal—underscored their commitment to their values and vision, making their leadership presence more compelling and authentic.

Furthermore, this consistency enhanced Alex's influence. By always aligning their communication with their leadership brand, they ensured that their message was not only heard but felt. It made their leadership not just visible but impactful, guiding their team towards shared goals and visions with coherence and clarity.

This strategic approach to communication allowed Alex to navigate the complexities of leadership with greater effectiveness. It facilitated not just the achievement of immediate project goals but also the broader vision of fostering an innovative, inclusive, and high-performing culture at InnovateTech. Through careful alignment of their communication with their leadership brand, Alex ensured that their professional identity was not just understood but respected and followed, setting a standard for leadership that was both inspiring and aspirational.

Consistency in both verbal and non-verbal communication is vital for reinforcing your leadership brand, contributing to trust, credibility, and a strong professional identity. Verbal communication should be clear, reliable, and aligned with your brand, enhancing your influence and persuasion. Similarly, non-verbal cues like body language, facial expressions, and professional appearance play a crucial role. Consistent communication builds trust through predictability and credibility through alignment, while enhancing leadership presence through authenticity and influence through consistency. By aligning communication with your leadership brand, you ensure clarity, coherence, and compelling professional identity, facilitating effective leadership and goal achievement.

Verbal Communication

1. **Clarity and Reliability**: Consistent verbal communication ensures that your message is clear and reliable, reducing misunderstandings and building trust among your team members and peers. When people know what to expect from you in communication, they're more likely to trust your leadership.
2. **Alignment with Leadership Brand**: The words you choose, the tone you adopt, and the messages you consistently convey should align with your leadership brand. For example, if your leadership brand emphasizes openness and transparency, consistently communicating in an open and honest manner reinforces this aspect of your brand.
3. **Influence and Persuasion**: Consistency in your messaging can enhance your ability to influence and persuade. When your verbal communication consistently reflects your values and vision, people are more likely to be persuaded by your arguments and follow your lead.

Non-Verbal Communication

1. **Body Language**: Non-verbal cues like eye contact, posture, and gestures can significantly impact how your leadership brand is perceived. Consistent positive body language can reinforce your confidence and authority, while inconsistency can undermine your message.
2. **Facial Expressions**: Expressions convey emotions and attitudes. Consistency in your facial expressions, aligned with your verbal

messages, enhances your authenticity and the emotional impact of your communication.
3. **Professional Appearance**: Your appearance is a form of non-verbal communication that can significantly affect how you're perceived. Dressing consistently in a manner that aligns with your leadership brand (whether it's authoritative, approachable, innovative, etc.) can reinforce the professional image you wish to project.

Building Trust and Credibility

- **Trust Through Predictability**: Consistency in communication, both verbal and non-verbal, makes you more predictable. This predictability allows team members to feel secure in their expectations, building trust over time.
- **Credibility Through Alignment**: When your verbal and non-verbal communications are consistently aligned with each other and with your stated values and goals, it enhances your credibility. People are more likely to believe in and follow a leader whose actions and words are in harmony.

Enhancing Leadership Presence

- **Presence Through Authenticity**: A consistent communication style that reflects your true self enhances your leadership presence. Authenticity makes you more relatable and respected as a leader.
- **Influence Through Consistency**: A consistent leadership brand, reinforced through both verbal and non-verbal communication, enhances your overall influence. People are more likely to be influenced by leaders who are consistent in their communication and behavior.

In summary, consistency in verbal and non-verbal communication is crucial for reinforcing your leadership brand. It builds trust, enhances your credibility, and strengthens your influence, making it easier for you to lead effectively and achieve your goals. By aligning your communication with your leadership brand, you ensure that your professional identity is clear, coherent, and compelling to those around you.

Fill in the Blank Questions:

1. Consistency in both verbal and _____ communication is pivotal for reinforcing your leadership brand.
2. Non-verbal cues like eye contact, posture, and gestures significantly impact how your _____ brand is perceived.
3. Trust is built through predictability, making you more _____ to your team members.

Multiple Choice Questions:

1. **How does consistency in verbal communication contribute to reinforcing your leadership brand?** A) By using complex language to impress team members B) By ensuring clarity and reliability in your message C) By frequently changing your tone and messages D) By avoiding verbal communication altogether
2. **Why is consistency in non-verbal communication important for leadership presence?** A) It adds confusion to your message B) It undermines your authenticity C) It reinforces your credibility and authority D) It demonstrates unpredictability
3. **What role does trust play in the context of consistency in communication?** A) It is unrelated to predictability B) It is built through consistent communication C) It is irrelevant in leadership D) It is undermined by credibility

Books:

1. "Talk Like TED: The 9 Public-Speaking Secrets of the World's Top Minds" by Carmine Gallo - This book provides valuable insights into effective verbal communication techniques, drawing from TED Talks by influential speakers. It offers practical tips for crafting clear, compelling messages that align with your leadership brand and enhance your influence.
2. "The Nonverbal Advantage: Secrets and Science of Body Language at Work" by Carol Kinsey Goman - Kinsey Goman

explores the impact of non-verbal communication on professional success, offering strategies for leveraging body language, facial expressions, and appearance to reinforce your leadership brand and build trust and credibility.
3. **"Executive Presence: The Art of Commanding Respect Like a CEO"** by Harrison Monarth - Monarth delves into the concept of executive presence and its importance in leadership success. The book provides guidance on how to align verbal and non-verbal communication with your leadership brand to project confidence, credibility, and influence.

Additional Resources:

1. **Communication Skills Workshops** - Participating in communication skills workshops tailored for leaders can help enhance both verbal and non-verbal communication abilities, providing practical techniques and exercises to strengthen your communication effectiveness and reinforce your leadership brand.
2. **Executive Coaching** - Working with an executive coach can provide personalized feedback and guidance on improving communication consistency and alignment with your leadership brand. Coaches can help identify areas for improvement and develop strategies for enhancing your overall communication impact.
3. **Peer Feedback and Role-Playing Exercises** - Engaging in peer feedback sessions and role-playing exercises allows leaders to receive constructive feedback on their communication style and practice aligning verbal and non-verbal cues with their leadership brand in a supportive environment, facilitating continuous improvement and refinement of communication skills.
4. **Online Resources and Webinars** - Various online resources and webinars focus on effective communication strategies for leaders, offering tips, best practices, and practical insights for aligning verbal and non-verbal communication with your leadership brand. Platforms like SkillPath, LinkedIn Learning, TED Talks, and industry-specific webinars provide accessible resources for ongoing skill development.

Chapter 5: Aligning Actions with Your Leadership Brand

Ensuring Alignment: Tips for Reflecting Your Leadership Brand and Core Values in Daily Actions and Interactions

Alex understood that authenticity was the bedrock of impactful leadership. Aware that actions speak louder than words, they were meticulous in ensuring their daily behaviors, decisions, and interactions mirrored the principles of their leadership brand. This commitment to authenticity began with a deep self-awareness, a trait Alex had cultivated over their journey. Regular reflection on their core values and the feedback received from peers, mentors, and team members served as a compass, helping Alex stay aligned with their leadership identity.

Each day, Alex set clear intentions, focusing on how they could embody their values of innovation, empathy, integrity, and inclusivity. This practice wasn't just about setting goals but about consciously planning how to interact, communicate, and make decisions in a way that reinforced their leadership brand. Whether it was a strategic meeting, a casual conversation with a team member, or a challenging decision that needed to be made, Alex strived for consistency, ensuring their actions reflected their leadership statement.

Leading by example was a principle Alex lived by. They knew that to inspire their team and foster a culture of innovation and inclusivity, they needed to be the embodiment of those values. This meant not shying away from difficult conversations, being transparent about challenges and failures, and showing vulnerability. Alex's transparency and willingness to share their learning journey encouraged a similar openness and growth mindset within their team.

Openness to learning and adaptation was another key aspect of Alex's leadership. The tech industry's fast-paced nature meant that change was the only constant, and Alex embraced this, viewing every challenge as an opportunity to learn and evolve. This adaptability not only enhanced Alex's leadership capabilities but also inspired their team to embrace change with confidence and curiosity.

Fostering genuine relationships was central to Alex's approach. They invested time in getting to know their team members, understanding their aspirations, challenges, and how they could support their growth. This investment went beyond professional mentorship; it was about building a community within InnovateTech where everyone felt valued and understood.

Mentorship was a role Alex took seriously, not just within their team but across the organization. They dedicated time to mentoring emerging leaders, sharing their insights, experiences, and the lessons they had learned. This commitment to developing others was a testament to Alex's belief in the power of collective growth and the impact of nurturing the next generation of leaders.

Regularly reflecting on and adjusting their approach was crucial for Alex. They recognized that leadership was a journey, not a destination. The feedback loops they had established, coupled with their reflective practices, ensured they remained responsive to their team's needs, industry trends, and their own growth as a leader.

Through these practices, Alex not only maintained authenticity and impact in their leadership but also deepened their influence within InnovateTech and the broader tech community. Their leadership journey was a testament to the power of authentic leadership, demonstrating that by staying true to one's values and brand, a leader could inspire change, drive innovation, and create a legacy of empowerment and growth.

Ensuring that your daily actions, decisions, and interactions reflect your leadership brand and core values is fundamental to authentic leadership. Starting with self-awareness, regularly reflecting on your values and seeking feedback from others helps maintain alignment. Setting clear intentions each day and practicing consistency in communication and decision-making further reinforces your leadership identity. Leading by example, embracing transparency, and staying open to learning and adaptation are essential. Additionally, fostering genuine relationships, offering mentorship, and regularly reflecting on and adjusting your approach contribute to maintaining authenticity and impact as a leader.

1. Start with Self-Awareness

- **Reflect Regularly**: Spend time regularly reflecting on your core values and leadership brand. Consider how well your recent actions and decisions have aligned with these principles.
- **Seek Feedback**: Regularly ask for feedback from peers, mentors, and team members on how they perceive your actions and whether they align with the values and brand you aim to represent.

2. Set Clear Intentions

- **Daily Goals**: Each morning, set clear intentions for how you want to embody your leadership brand throughout the day. This could involve specific behaviors, communication styles, or decision-making approaches that reflect your core values.
- **Visual Reminders**: Keep visual reminders of your core values and leadership brand in your workspace. This could be a simple note, a desktop wallpaper, or any symbolic item that keeps your leadership identity at the forefront of your mind.

3. Practice Consistency

- **Consistent Communication**: Ensure your verbal and written communications consistently reflect your leadership brand. Whether it's an email, a meeting, or a social media post, use language that aligns with your core values.
- **Align Decisions with Values**: Before making decisions, ask yourself if they align with your core values and leadership brand.

This consistency in decision-making reinforces your leadership identity.

4. Lead by Example

- **Model Behaviors**: Be a living example of your leadership brand. Demonstrate the behaviors and attitudes you wish to see in your team. Leading by example is one of the most powerful ways to reinforce your leadership brand.
- **Embrace Transparency**: When making decisions or taking actions, be transparent about your rationale, especially when they are directly tied to your core values. This helps others understand and align with your leadership approach.

5. Adapt and Evolve

- **Stay Open to Learning**: Your leadership brand should evolve as you grow and learn. Stay open to new experiences and feedback that can shape your leadership style and values.
- **Adapt Flexibly**: While staying true to your core values, be flexible in how you express your leadership brand. Different situations may call for different aspects of your leadership identity to come to the forefront.

6. Foster Relationships

- **Build Genuine Connections**: Invest time in building relationships with your team members and peers. Genuine connections allow for deeper understanding and communication, making it easier to express your leadership brand authentically.
- **Mentorship and Coaching**: Offer mentorship and coaching to others. This not only allows you to directly impart your values and brand but also strengthens your leadership identity through the act of teaching and guiding others.

7. Reflect and Adjust

- **Regular Review**: End each day or week with a review of how well your actions and decisions have reflected your leadership brand. Consider what went well and what could be improved.
- **Responsive Adjustments**: Be willing to adjust based on your reflections and feedback from others. Continuous improvement is key to maintaining an authentic and impactful leadership brand.

By integrating these practices into your daily routine, you can ensure that your leadership brand is not just a concept but a living part of how you lead every day. This alignment between your actions, decisions, and leadership identity enhances your effectiveness as a leader and strengthens the trust and credibility you build with others.

Fill in the Blank:

1. Regularly asking for feedback from peers, mentors, and team members helps in assessing how well your actions align with your _____.
2. Keeping visual reminders of your core values and leadership brand in your workspace helps in keeping your leadership identity at the _____ of your mind.
3. Before making decisions, it's crucial to ask yourself if they align with your core values and _____.

Multiple Choice:

1. **What is one way to ensure consistency in communication with your leadership brand?** A) Using different language styles in different contexts B) Ensuring your verbal and written communications align with your core values C) Avoiding communication altogether D) Communicating only with a select group of individuals
2. **How can leading by example reinforce your leadership brand?** A) By being inconsistent in your behaviors B) By demonstrating the behaviors and attitudes you wish to see in

your team C) By delegating tasks without being involved D) By keeping your decisions opaque
3. **Why is it important to stay open to learning and adaptation in leadership?** A) To remain static and unchanging in your approach B) To limit growth opportunities for yourself and your team C) To ensure your leadership brand evolves as you grow and learn D) To avoid feedback and mentorship

Books:

1. "**Dare to Lead: Brave Work. Tough Conversations. Whole Hearts**." by Brené Brown - Brené Brown explores the qualities of authentic leadership, emphasizing vulnerability, courage, and integrity. The book provides practical guidance on how leaders can align their actions with their values and cultivate trust within their teams.
2. "**Authentic Leadership: Rediscovering the Secrets to Creating Lasting Value**" by Bill George - Bill George delves into the concept of authentic leadership, drawing on interviews with leaders from various fields. He outlines a framework for developing authentic leadership based on self-awareness, values, and genuine relationships.
3. "**Leaders Eat Last: Why Some Teams Pull Together and Others Don't**" by Simon Sinek - Simon Sinek discusses the importance of leaders embodying their values and prioritizing the well-being of their teams. The book explores how authentic leadership fosters trust, collaboration, and organizational success.

Additional Resources:

1. **Leadership Retreats and Workshops** - Participating in leadership retreats and workshops focused on authenticity and values-based leadership can provide opportunities for self-reflection, skill-building, and peer learning in a supportive environment.
2. **Leadership Development Programs** - Enrolling in leadership development programs that incorporate modules on authenticity and self-awareness can help leaders deepen their understanding

of their core values and how they translate into authentic leadership practices.
3. **Executive Coaching** - Working with an executive coach specializing in authentic leadership can provide personalized guidance and support in aligning daily actions with core values, fostering authenticity, and maximizing leadership impact.
4. **Online Courses and Webinars** - Various online courses and webinars address topics related to authentic leadership, offering insights and strategies for maintaining alignment with core values in daily leadership practices. Platforms like Coursera, Udemy, and TED Talks feature relevant resources for ongoing development.

Embracing Authenticity and Integrity: Pillars of Living Your Leadership Brand

Alex's journey of embodying their leadership brand with authenticity and integrity had become a cornerstone of their identity at InnovateTech. They understood that to inspire confidence, foster loyalty, and lead effectively, they needed to be seen as genuine and trustworthy by their team members, peers, and the broader organizational network.

Embracing transparency, Alex was open about their values, beliefs, and even their shortcomings. This honesty did more than just foster trust; it enhanced engagement among their team members. By sharing their challenges and how they were working to overcome them, Alex made it clear that it was okay to be imperfect. This level of vulnerability facilitated deeper connections, encouraging team members to be open about their own experiences and areas for growth.

Moreover, Alex's commitment to integrity was unwavering. They led by example, making decisions that were not only effective but ethical. This approach established a culture of credibility within their team, promoting ethical behavior across all levels of interaction. When faced with tough choices, Alex's team knew they could look to their leader for guidance that was not just strategic but morally sound.

To continuously embody these qualities, Alex engaged in regular self-reflection. They set aside time each week to consider their actions and decisions, assessing whether they were in alignment with their core values of integrity and authenticity. This practice ensured that they remained grounded in their leadership brand, even when faced with the rapid pace of change and pressure inherent in the tech industry.

Transparent communication was another strategy Alex employed. They made it a priority to communicate clearly and openly with their team, not just about goals and expectations but about the reasoning behind decisions and the vision driving the team forward. This openness ensured that everyone was on the same page, reducing misunderstandings and fostering a culture of inclusivity and collaboration.

Consistent behavior was crucial. Alex knew that trust was built through consistency, so they made every effort to ensure their actions always reflected their leadership principles. Whether in a high-stakes meeting or a casual conversation, Alex's team could expect the same level of respect, empathy, and commitment to excellence.

Accountability was perhaps the most challenging aspect of living their leadership brand, but Alex embraced it fully. They held themselves accountable for their actions, celebrating successes with their team and taking responsibility for setbacks. This accountability extended to their team as well, creating an environment where everyone was encouraged to take ownership of their work and learn from their experiences.

Through these practices, Alex not only reinforced their leadership brand but also contributed to a positive organizational culture at InnovateTech. The result was a more engaged and committed team, one that was not only productive but also shared a deep sense of loyalty and respect for their leader. Alex's journey demonstrated that authenticity and integrity are not just personal virtues but foundational pillars for effective leadership, capable of transforming teams and organizations from the inside out.

Authenticity and integrity serve as foundational pillars for living your leadership brand, ensuring that your leadership is perceived as genuine and trustworthy, which is crucial for inspiring confidence and loyalty among your team members and peers. Authentic leaders are transparent about their values, beliefs, and shortcomings, fostering trust, enhancing engagement, facilitating connection, and driving consistency. Similarly, leaders with integrity establish credibility, promote ethical behavior, support decision-making, and foster respect. To embody these qualities, leaders can engage in self-reflection, transparent communication, consistent behavior, and accountability. This approach not only enhances their leadership brand but also contributes to a positive organizational culture and a more engaged and committed team.

Authenticity

- **Builds Trust**: Authentic leaders are transparent about their values, beliefs, and shortcomings. This openness fosters trust, as team members feel they are following someone genuine and human.
- **Enhances Engagement**: When leaders are authentic, they create an environment where their team members feel comfortable being themselves. This can lead to increased engagement, creativity, and job satisfaction.
- **Facilitates Connection**: Authenticity allows leaders to connect with their team on a personal level. This connection is vital for building strong relationships that can withstand challenges and conflicts.
- **Drives Consistency**: An authentic leadership brand is consistent; it doesn't shift based on circumstances. This consistency helps in setting clear expectations for the team and provides a stable leadership presence that people can rely on.

Integrity

- **Establishes Credibility**: Leaders with integrity act in alignment with their values and promises. This consistency between words and actions establishes the leader's credibility and reliability.
- **Promotes Ethical Behavior**: Integrity in leadership encourages a culture of ethics and fairness within the team and organization. Leaders who demonstrate integrity set the standard for ethical behavior among their team members.
- **Supports Decision Making**: Integrity guides leaders in making fair and balanced decisions, even in difficult situations. It ensures that decisions are made based on values and principles, rather than convenience or personal gain.
- **Fosters Respect**: Leaders who demonstrate integrity earn the respect of their team members and peers. Respect is crucial for effective leadership, as it enhances the leader's influence and effectiveness.

Living Your Leadership Brand with Authenticity and Integrity

To embody these qualities in your leadership practice, consider the following actions:

- **Self-Reflection**: Regularly reflect on your values, ensuring your actions and decisions align with these core principles.
- **Transparent Communication**: Be open and honest in your communications, sharing not only successes but also acknowledging failures and lessons learned.
- **Consistent Behavior**: Ensure that your actions consistently reflect your leadership brand, regardless of the situation. This means making tough decisions that align with your values, even when they are not the easiest or most popular choices.
- **Accountability**: Hold yourself accountable for your actions and decisions. When mistakes happen, own up to them, learn from them, and make amends where necessary.

Authenticity and integrity in leadership are not just about maintaining a positive image; they are about being true to yourself and leading in a way that is respectful, ethical, and genuine. This approach not only enhances your leadership brand but also contributes to a positive organizational culture and a more engaged and committed team.

Fill in the Blank:

1. Authentic leaders are transparent about their _____, beliefs, and shortcomings.
2. Integrity in leadership encourages a culture of _____ and fairness within the team and organization.
3. To embody authenticity and integrity, leaders can engage in self-_____.
4. Leaders with integrity establish credibility by acting in alignment with their values and _____.

Multiple Choice:

1. **What is one benefit of authenticity in leadership?** A) Creating a secretive environment B) Fostering trust among team members C) Encouraging disengagement D) Promoting dishonesty
2. **How does integrity support decision-making in leadership?** A) By making decisions based on convenience B) By guiding leaders to make fair and balanced decisions C) By encouraging unethical behavior D) By ignoring values and principles
3. **Why is transparent communication important for authenticity in leadership?** A) To hide failures and mistakes B) To foster trust and connection C) To discourage engagement D) To promote secrecy
4. **What role does consistency play in living your leadership brand?** A) It creates confusion among team members B) It fosters an environment of uncertainty C) It sets clear expectations for the team D) It encourages unpredictable behavior

Books:

1. **"The Authenticity Principle: Resist Conformity, Embrace Differences, and Transform How You Live, Work, and Lead"** by Ritu Bhasin - Ritu Bhasin explores the importance of authenticity in leadership and provides actionable strategies for embracing authenticity in both personal and professional life. The book offers insights into overcoming barriers to authenticity and building trust with others.
2. **"Integrity: The Courage to Meet the Demands of Reality"** by Henry Cloud - Henry Cloud discusses the significance of integrity in leadership and life, emphasizing the importance of aligning actions with values. The book provides practical guidance on developing and maintaining integrity, fostering trust, and building strong relationships.
3. **"Leadership and Self-Deception: Getting Out of the Box"** by The Arbinger Institute - This book offers a unique perspective on authenticity and leadership by exploring the concept of self-deception. It examines how leaders can overcome self-deception to lead with authenticity, integrity, and empathy.

Additional Resources:

1. **Authentic Leadership Development Programs** - Participating in leadership development programs focused on authenticity can provide leaders with tools and techniques to cultivate authenticity in their leadership style. These programs often include workshops, coaching sessions, and peer learning opportunities.
2. **Ethical Leadership Training** - Enrolling in ethical leadership training courses can help leaders understand the importance of integrity in leadership and develop strategies for making ethical decisions in challenging situations. Organizations like the Ethics & Compliance Initiative offer resources and training programs on ethical leadership.
3. **Authenticity Assessments and Feedback Tools** - Utilizing authenticity assessments and feedback tools can help leaders gain insight into their authentic leadership style and areas for improvement. Tools like the Authentic Leadership Questionnaire

(ALQ) and 360-degree feedback surveys can provide valuable feedback from colleagues, peers, and direct reports.
4. **Leadership Retreats and Workshops** - Attending leadership retreats and workshops focused on authenticity and integrity can offer leaders opportunities for self-reflection, skill-building, and networking with like-minded individuals. These events often feature discussions, exercises, and guest speakers sharing insights on authentic leadership practices.

Chapter 6: Building and Maintaining Your Network

Building Your Professional Network: Guidance for Expanding and Nurturing a Supportive Ecosystem for Your Leadership Brand

Alex recognized the power of a strong professional network in amplifying their leadership brand and furthering their impact within and beyond InnovateTech. They approached networking with the same intentionality and strategic thinking that had guided their leadership journey thus far.

First, Alex defined their networking goals with clarity, ensuring these objectives were well-aligned with their leadership brand and professional aspirations. This clarity helped them identify which events to attend, whom to connect with, and what kind of content to share and engage with.

Optimizing their LinkedIn profile was a key step. Alex updated their profile to reflect their leadership brand statement, showcasing their values, vision, and achievements. They made sure their profile was not just a resume but a narrative that communicated their leadership journey and aspirations.

Active engagement on professional platforms became part of Alex's routine. They participated in discussions, shared insights, and commented on posts that resonated with their brand. This engagement helped Alex stay visible and relevant within their professional community.

Attending industry events, both virtually and in-person, allowed Alex to connect with like-minded professionals and leaders. They chose events that were aligned with their values and areas of expertise, using these opportunities to learn, share insights, and foster new connections.

Creating valuable content was another strategy Alex employed. They wrote articles and shared posts on topics related to innovation, leadership, and team culture, contributing to conversations that mattered in their industry. This not only reinforced Alex's brand but also positioned them as a thought leader.

Fostering genuine connections was at the heart of Alex's networking strategy. They approached each interaction with curiosity and empathy, seeking to understand the other person's interests and challenges. This genuine interest helped Alex build deeper, more meaningful relationships.

Seeking and providing mentorship was a dual pathway for growth. Alex connected with mentors who could offer guidance and support, and they also made themselves available to mentor others, sharing their knowledge and experiences generously.

Engaging in continuous learning was essential for Alex to stay relevant and informed. They attended workshops, webinars, and conferences, often sharing key takeaways with their network, which sparked further discussions and learning opportunities.

Utilizing social media wisely, Alex was careful to curate their online presence, sharing and engaging with content that reflected their leadership identity and professional interests. This careful curation helped maintain the coherence of their brand across platforms.

Giving back to the community through volunteering was another way Alex expanded their network. They participated in initiatives that aligned with their values, such as mentoring programs for young professionals and tech education for underrepresented groups. This not only broadened their network but also enriched their sense of purpose and contribution.

Maintaining patience and persistence in building relationships was perhaps the most crucial strategy. Alex knew that meaningful connections couldn't be rushed and that their network would grow in value and strength over time.

Through these strategies, Alex not only expanded their professional network but also ensured it was a robust support system that reinforced their leadership brand and contributed significantly to their professional growth and impact.

Expanding and nurturing a professional network is essential for reinforcing and amplifying your leadership brand. Strategies include identifying networking goals that align with your brand, optimizing your LinkedIn profile, actively engaging on professional platforms, attending relevant industry events, creating valuable content, fostering genuine connections, seeking and providing mentorship, engaging in continuous learning, utilizing social media wisely, giving back to your community through volunteering, and maintaining patience and persistence in building relationships. These strategies ensure that your network supports your leadership aspirations and contributes to your professional growth.

1. Identify Your Networking Goals

- **Align with Your Leadership Brand**: Clearly define what you hope to achieve through your networking efforts. Ensure these goals resonate with your leadership brand, whether it's finding mentorship opportunities, sharing knowledge, or collaborating on projects.

2. Leverage LinkedIn and Other Professional Platforms

- **Optimize Your Profile**: Ensure your LinkedIn profile reflects your leadership brand, highlighting your experiences, skills, and the value you bring to your network.
- **Active Engagement**: Regularly share content, comment on posts, and participate in discussions that align with your

leadership brand. This positions you as a thought leader in your area.

3. Attend Industry Events and Conferences

- **Selective Participation**: Choose events that are relevant to your industry and leadership interests. These gatherings are excellent opportunities to meet like-minded professionals.
- **Volunteer to Speak or Lead Sessions**: Sharing your expertise at these events can significantly enhance your visibility and establish your authority in the field.

4. Create and Share Valuable Content

- **Blog Posts or Articles**: Write about topics that showcase your leadership perspective and expertise. Share these on LinkedIn, industry forums, or your personal blog.
- **Host Webinars or Podcasts**: Organizing online events on topics of interest to your network can attract a broader audience and foster deeper connections.

5. Foster Genuine Connections

- **Quality Over Quantity**: Focus on building meaningful relationships rather than amassing many connections. Genuine interest and engagement will lead to a more supportive network.
- **Follow-up and Follow Through**: After meeting new contacts, follow up with a personalized message. Stay in touch by sharing information of mutual interest and helping when possible.

6. Seek Out and Provide Mentorship

- **Mentorship Relationships**: Both being a mentor and finding a mentor can enrich your professional network. These relationships can provide guidance, feedback, and new opportunities.
- **Peer Mentoring**: Forming peer mentoring groups can also be beneficial for mutual growth and accountability.

7. Engage in Continuous Learning and Development

- **Join Professional Associations**: Being part of professional groups or associations related to your field can offer networking opportunities and resources for professional development.
- **Participate in Workshops and Courses**: Continuous learning not only enhances your skills but also puts you in contact with professionals who share your interests.

8. Utilize Social Media Wisely

- **Consistent Branding Across Platforms**: Ensure your social media profiles across different platforms consistently reflect your leadership brand. This coherence strengthens your professional image.
- **Interactive Engagement**: Use social media not just for broadcasting your achievements but for engaging with others' content in a meaningful way.

9. Give Back to Your Community

- **Volunteer**: Offer your time and skills to community projects or non-profit organizations. This can broaden your network to include individuals outside your immediate industry, enriching your professional and personal life.

10. Be Patient and Persistent

- **Long-term Perspective**: Building a strong professional network is a long-term endeavor. Be patient and maintain a consistent effort in nurturing your connections.

By following these strategies, you can build a professional network that not only supports your current leadership role but also contributes to your future growth. Remember, the key to a successful network is not just in its size but in the quality and depth of the relationships you cultivate.

Fill in the Blank:

1. Ensure these goals resonate with your leadership _____.
2. Regularly share content, comment on posts, and participate in discussions that align with your leadership _____.
3. Both being a mentor and finding a mentor can enrich your professional _____.
4. Building a strong professional network is a long-term _____.

Multiple Choice:

1. **Why is it important to attend industry events and conferences for networking?** A) To socialize with friends B) To amass a large number of connections C) To meet like-minded professionals D) To avoid networking opportunities
2. **What should be the focus when building a professional network?** A) Quantity over quality B) Building meaningful relationships C) Avoiding genuine connections D) Staying isolated from the professional community
3. **How can one utilize social media for networking?** A) By only broadcasting achievements B) By consistently engaging with others' content C) By remaining passive on the platforms D) By avoiding any interaction with others
4. **Why is it important to give back to your community for networking?** A) To isolate oneself from others B) To limit professional growth C) To broaden your network D) To avoid building meaningful relationships

Books:

1. **"Never Eat Alone: And Other Secrets to Success, One Relationship at a Time"** by Keith Ferrazzi - Keith Ferrazzi shares strategies for building and nurturing professional relationships to advance your career and personal goals. The book provides actionable tips for networking effectively and leveraging relationships to amplify your leadership brand.

2. **"Give and Take: Why Helping Others Drives Our Success"** by Adam Grant - Adam Grant explores the power of networking and generosity in achieving success. The book examines different approaches to networking and highlights the benefits of giving back to others in building a strong professional network.
3. **"The Connector's Advantage: 7 Mindsets to Grow Your Influence and Impact"** by Michelle Tillis Lederman - Michelle Tillis Lederman discusses the mindset and strategies of effective connectors who build meaningful relationships and expand their influence. The book offers practical advice for networking with authenticity and purpose.

Additional Resources:

1. **Networking Events and Conferences** - Attending networking events and industry conferences provides opportunities to meet new people, exchange ideas, and build connections within your field. Look for events relevant to your interests and leadership goals.
2. **Online Networking Groups and Communities** - Joining online networking groups and communities on platforms like LinkedIn or industry-specific forums allows you to connect with professionals worldwide, share insights, and participate in discussions relevant to your leadership brand.
3. **Networking Workshops and Training** - Participating in networking workshops and training sessions can help you refine your networking skills, overcome challenges, and develop effective strategies for building and maintaining professional relationships.
4. **Networking Apps and Tools** - Utilizing networking apps and tools can streamline the networking process and help you manage your contacts more efficiently. Apps like Shapr, Bizzabo, and Meetup can facilitate networking opportunities and connect you with like-minded professionals in your area or industry.

Unlocking Leadership Potential: Harnessing Mentorship for Personal Growth and Development

Alex's commitment to mentorship was both a personal and professional calling. Having experienced the transformative impact of mentorship on their own journey, Alex was eager to foster these relationships, understanding the reciprocal value for both mentors and mentees.

As a mentee, Alex had sought out mentors who could provide not just guidance but also challenge them to grow beyond their comfort zones. These mentors accelerated Alex's learning, offering insights drawn from years of experience that Alex could apply in real-time. The personalized feedback received was invaluable, pinpointing areas for improvement in a way that was constructive and empowering. This mentorship also expanded Alex's professional network, connecting them with individuals and opportunities they might not have encountered otherwise. Importantly, these relationships enhanced Alex's confidence, equipping them to take on new challenges and ambitious projects. Goal setting and career planning became a collaborative effort, with mentors providing a sounding board for Alex's aspirations.

In turn, as a mentor, Alex found the role deeply rewarding. It allowed them to refine their leadership skills, especially in coaching, listening, and providing feedback. The need for self-reflection was heightened, as Alex sought to offer the best guidance while navigating the nuances of their mentees' challenges and goals. This role offered a profound sense of professional satisfaction, stemming from the ability to contribute to someone else's growth and success. Sharing their knowledge and experiences was not just about teaching but about learning through the act of mentoring. Engaging with mentees from diverse backgrounds and with varied aspirations also expanded Alex's perspectives, challenging them to think differently and embrace new ideas.

For these mentorship relationships to be fruitful, Alex knew that both parties needed to establish clear objectives from the outset. This clarity ensured that their interactions were purposeful and aligned with their respective goals. Open communication was vital, creating a space where feedback could be exchanged freely and challenges discussed openly. Mutual respect was the foundation of these relationships, acknowledging the value and contributions of both mentor and mentee. Above all, a commitment to growth was essential, with both Alex and their mentees entering the relationship with a mindset geared towards continuous learning and development.

These mentorship relationships did more than just contribute to individual career success; they fostered a culture of learning and development within InnovateTech and the broader professional community. Alex's engagement in mentorship underscored the belief that leadership is not just about achieving personal success but about lifting others as you climb. Through mentorship, Alex not only amplified their impact as a leader but also contributed to building a legacy of leadership development that would endure well beyond their tenure.

Mentorship is a cornerstone of leadership development, providing numerous benefits for both mentors and mentees. As a mentee, engaging with a mentor accelerates learning, provides personalized feedback, expands professional networks, enhances confidence, and aids in goal setting and career planning. Meanwhile, mentors refine their leadership skills, increase self-reflection, find professional satisfaction, share knowledge, and gain expanded perspectives. Both parties should establish clear objectives, maintain open communication, uphold mutual respect, and commit to growth for a fruitful mentorship. These relationships foster continuous learning and contribute to overall career success.

As a Mentee

1. **Accelerated Learning**: Being a mentee allows you to learn from the experiences, mistakes, and successes of seasoned leaders.

This can accelerate your learning curve and help you avoid common pitfalls.
2. **Personalized Feedback**: Regular feedback from a mentor can provide you with insights into your leadership style, strengths, and areas for improvement that are difficult to gain from other sources.
3. **Expanded Professional Network**: A mentor can introduce you to their professional network, providing opportunities for networking and exposure to new ideas and perspectives.
4. **Enhanced Confidence**: The support and encouragement from a mentor can boost your confidence in making decisions and taking on leadership challenges.
5. **Goal Setting and Career Planning**: Mentors can assist in setting realistic career goals and developing strategies to achieve them, helping you navigate your career path more effectively.

As a Mentor

1. **Refined Leadership Skills**: The act of mentoring others requires and hones key leadership skills such as communication, empathy, and the ability to motivate and inspire others.
2. **Increased Self-Reflection**: Serving as a mentor encourages self-reflection as you share your experiences and advice, helping you to identify your own strengths and weaknesses as a leader.
3. **Professional Satisfaction and Legacy Building**: Mentoring allows you to give back to your profession by guiding emerging leaders, contributing to your sense of professional fulfillment and leaving a lasting impact on your industry.
4. **Knowledge Sharing and Relevance**: Teaching others helps you consolidate your own knowledge and stay updated on new trends and perspectives, ensuring your own continuous learning and relevance in your field.
5. **Expanded Perspective**: Engaging with mentees can expose you to new ideas, challenges, and viewpoints, broadening your perspective and fostering a culture of learning and innovation.

Maximizing the Benefits of Mentorship

- **Clear Objectives**: Both mentors and mentees should enter the relationship with clear objectives and expectations to ensure a productive partnership.
- **Open Communication**: A successful mentorship relies on open, honest communication. Regular check-ins and feedback are essential.
- **Mutual Respect**: Both parties should respect each other's time, commitment, and contributions to the mentorship relationship.
- **Commitment to Growth**: Both mentors and mentees should be committed to personal and professional growth, embracing challenges and learning opportunities.

Mentorship is a two-way street, offering valuable opportunities for learning and growth on both sides. Whether you're seeking guidance as a mentee or offering insight as a mentor, these relationships can significantly enhance your leadership development and contribute to your overall career success.

Fill in the Blank:

1. Mentors can introduce you to their _____, providing opportunities for networking.
2. The act of mentoring others requires and hones key leadership _____ such as communication and empathy.
3. A successful mentorship relies on open, honest _____.
4. Both mentors and mentees should be committed to personal and professional _____.

Multiple Choice:

1. **What does mentorship offer for both mentors and mentees?**
A) Personal growth only B) Benefits only for mentees C) Significant benefits D) Isolation from professional networks

2. **What is a benefit of being a mentee?** A) Decreased confidence B) Limited learning opportunities C) Expanded professional network D) Reduced goal setting
3. **What should both mentors and mentees establish for a productive mentorship?** A) Ambiguity B) Clear objectives C) Inconsistency D) Lack of commitment
4. **What is the benefit of being a mentor?** A) Decreased self-reflection B) Limited knowledge sharing C) Increased professional satisfaction D) Isolation from new ideas

Books:

1. "**The Mentor's Guide: Facilitating Effective Learning Relationships**" by Lois J. Zachary - This book provides practical guidance for mentors, offering strategies for fostering effective learning relationships, providing feedback, and supporting mentees in their professional development journey.
2. "**The Power of Mentoring: Shaping People Who Will Shape the World**" by Martin Sanders - Martin Sanders explores the transformative impact of mentoring relationships on individuals and organizations. The book offers insights into the mentorship process and how mentors can empower mentees to reach their full potential.
3. "**One Minute Mentoring: How to Find and Work With a Mentor - and Why You'll Benefit from Being One**" by Ken Blanchard and Claire Diaz-Ortiz - Ken Blanchard and Claire Diaz-Ortiz present a practical guide to mentorship, emphasizing the importance of mentorship in personal and professional growth. The book provides tips for finding a mentor, building a successful mentoring relationship, and becoming a mentor yourself.

Additional Resources:

1. **Mentorship Programs and Organizations** - Many organizations offer formal mentorship programs that pair mentors with mentees based on their interests, goals, and areas of expertise. Research mentorship programs in your industry or community to find opportunities for mentorship.

2. **Mentorship Workshops and Training** - Participating in mentorship workshops and training sessions can enhance your mentorship skills and prepare you for effective mentorship relationships. Look for workshops offered by professional associations, educational institutions, or leadership development organizations.
3. **Mentorship Networking Events** - Attend networking events focused on mentorship to connect with potential mentors or mentees and learn from experienced professionals in your field. These events provide opportunities to build relationships and explore mentorship opportunities in a supportive environment.
4. **Online Mentorship Platforms** - Utilize online mentorship platforms and networks to connect with mentors and mentees beyond your immediate geographic location. Websites like MentorCity, iCouldBe, and LinkedIn offer platforms for finding mentorship opportunities and connecting with professionals who share your interests and goals.

Chapter 7: Continuous Learning and Adaptation

Embracing Lifelong Learning: Strategies for Evolving Your Leadership Brand Over Time

Alex embraced continuous learning as a crucial component of their leadership evolution. Recognizing that the landscape of technology and leadership was perpetually shifting, Alex committed to strategies that ensured their growth and adaptation over time.

Embracing a growth mindset was foundational. Alex stayed curious, seeing every challenge as an opportunity to learn and every failure as a steppingstone to success. This mindset encouraged resilience, allowing Alex to navigate the ups and downs of leading in a high-paced industry with grace and determination.

Setting SMART (Specific, Measurable, Achievable, Relevant, Time-bound) learning goals helped Alex focus their efforts. Whether it was mastering a new technology, improving their emotional intelligence, or understanding global market trends, these goals provided a clear direction for their learning journey.

Leveraging formal education and training, Alex attended leadership development programs and workshops that were directly aligned with their aspirations and challenges. These structured learning opportunities provided deep dives into specific topics, enriching Alex's understanding and skills.

Utilizing online resources became a daily habit for Alex. They subscribed to leadership podcasts, enrolled in online courses relevant to their industry, and participated in webinars. These resources offered flexibility, allowing Alex to learn at their own pace and on their own schedule.

Engaging in peer learning through mastermind groups and mentorship was particularly enriching. These forums provided a space for sharing challenges, strategies, and insights with peers and mentors, fostering a collaborative learning environment that broadened Alex's perspectives.

Reading widely, from leadership books to industry publications, kept Alex informed and inspired. They dedicated time each week to reading, ensuring they were exposed to new ideas and best practices that could inform their leadership approach.

Reflecting on experiences was a critical learning strategy for Alex. They maintained a reflective journal, documenting their challenges, successes, and the lessons learned along the way. This reflection turned experiences into valuable learning opportunities, deepening Alex's understanding of their leadership style and impact.

Staying informed on global trends ensured that Alex's leadership approach remained relevant and forward-thinking. They followed thought leaders and influencers in their field, keeping abreast of emerging trends and innovations that could impact their team and organization.

Networking was not just about expanding Alex's professional circle but also about learning from the diverse experiences and viewpoints of others. Engaging in meaningful conversations with individuals from different backgrounds and industries enriched Alex's learning and provided fresh insights.

Prioritizing self-care was a crucial aspect of Alex's continuous learning strategy. Recognizing that physical and mental well-being were essential for sustained growth and performance, Alex incorporated regular exercise, mindfulness practices, and hobbies that provided rest and rejuvenation into their routine.

These strategies collectively ensured that Alex's leadership brand remained dynamic, relevant, and effective. Continuous learning was not just about acquiring new knowledge but about translating that knowledge into actionable strategies that fostered growth, innovation, and adaptability. By committing to ongoing development, Alex not only enhanced their leadership brand but also contributed to the growth and success of their team and organization.

Continuous learning is integral to evolving and adapting your leadership brand over time. Approaches to ensure ongoing development include embracing a growth mindset by staying curious and learning from failures, setting SMART learning goals, leveraging formal education and training, utilizing online resources like courses and podcasts, engaging in peer learning through mastermind groups and mentorship, reading widely from leadership books and industry publications, reflecting on experiences, staying informed on global trends, networking, and prioritizing self-care. These strategies enable leaders to refine their brand dynamically, ensuring its relevance and effectiveness in addressing organizational and team needs. Continuous learning is not just about acquiring knowledge but also about translating it into actionable strategies that foster growth and innovation.

1. Embrace a Growth Mindset

- **Stay Curious**: Cultivate a curiosity for new knowledge and experiences. This mindset encourages ongoing learning and openness to change.
- **Learn from Failures**: View failures as learning opportunities. Reflect on what went wrong and how you can improve in the future.

2. Set Learning Goals

- **Identify Areas for Development**: Regularly assess your leadership skills and identify areas where you can improve or new skills you can acquire.

- **SMART Learning Goals**: Set specific, measurable, achievable, relevant, and time-bound (SMART) goals for your learning to keep you focused and motivated.

3. Leverage Formal Education and Training

- **Leadership Courses and Workshops**: Enroll in courses and workshops that focus on emerging leadership theories, strategies, and skills.
- **Professional Certifications**: Pursue certifications relevant to your industry or leadership level to enhance your credibility and knowledge base.

4. Utilize Online Resources

- **Online Courses**: Platforms like Coursera, edX, and LinkedIn Learning offer a wide range of courses on leadership and management topics.
- **Podcasts and Webinars**: Listen to leadership podcasts and attend webinars to gain insights from thought leaders across various industries.

5. Engage in Peer Learning

- **Mastermind Groups**: Join or form a mastermind group with peers who are also committed to leadership development. These groups provide a platform for sharing challenges, solutions, and learning from each other.
- **Mentorship**: Engage in mentorship relationships, both as a mentor and a mentee. This reciprocal learning relationship can offer fresh perspectives and insights.

6. Read Widely

- **Leadership Books**: Regularly read books on leadership and management. Aim to read from a diverse range of authors to gain multiple perspectives.

- **Industry Publications**: Stay updated with your industry's trends and challenges by reading relevant publications, journals, and articles.

7. Reflect and Apply

- **Reflective Practice**: Regularly reflect on your leadership experiences. Journaling about your challenges, successes, and lessons learned can deepen your understanding and application of new knowledge.
- **Apply Learning**: Actively apply what you learn in real-world situations. Experiment with new approaches and strategies to see what works best for you and your team.

8. Stay Informed on Global Trends

- **Global Awareness**: Stay informed about global economic, technological, and social trends. Understanding these broader trends can help you anticipate changes and adapt your leadership approach accordingly.

9. Network and Collaborate

- **Expand Your Network**: Regularly engage with professionals outside your immediate circle. Networking can expose you to new ideas, strategies, and best practices in leadership.

10. Prioritize Self-Care

- **Balance and Well-being**: Ensure that your commitment to continuous learning doesn't come at the expense of your well-being. Balancing professional development with physical and mental health is crucial for sustainable leadership.

Incorporating these approaches into your leadership journey allows you to continually refine your leadership brand, ensuring it remains dynamic, relevant, and effective in meeting the evolving needs of your organization and team. Continuous learning is not just about acquiring new knowledge but about transforming that knowledge into action that drives growth and innovation.

Fill in the Blank:

1. Embrace a growth mindset by cultivating a curiosity for new knowledge and _____.
2. Regularly assess your leadership skills and identify areas where you can improve or acquire new _____.
3. Utilize online resources such as Coursera, edX, and LinkedIn Learning to access a wide range of leadership _____.
4. Join or form a mastermind group with peers committed to leadership development to share challenges, solutions, and _____.

Multiple Choice:

1. **What is a key aspect of setting learning goals?** A) Vague objectives B) SMART criteria C) Random selection D) Unattainable targets
2. **How can leaders utilize formal education and training?** A) Avoiding courses and workshops B) Pursuing certifications C) Ignoring industry trends D) Rejecting online resources
3. **How can peer learning be facilitated?** A) Through isolation B) With mentorship only C) By engaging in mastermind groups D) Without feedback
4. **Why is reflecting on experiences important?** A) It wastes time B) It doesn't contribute to growth C) It deepens understanding D) It avoids learning opportunities

Books:

1. **"Mindset: The New Psychology of Success"** by Carol S. Dweck - Carol Dweck explores the concept of growth mindset and its implications for personal and professional development. The book offers insights into how adopting a growth mindset

can enhance leadership effectiveness and promote continuous learning.
2. **"The Fifth Discipline: The Art & Practice of The Learning Organization"** by Peter M. Senge - Peter Senge introduces the concept of the learning organization and presents principles for fostering continuous learning and innovation within organizations. The book provides frameworks and strategies for leaders to create environments that support ongoing learning and development.
3. **"Leaders Eat Last: Why Some Teams Pull Together and Others Don't"** by Simon Sinek - Simon Sinek explores the dynamics of effective leadership and teamwork, emphasizing the importance of continuous learning and personal growth for leaders. The book offers insights into building cultures of trust, collaboration, and continuous improvement.

Additional Resources:

1. **Online Learning Platforms** - Platforms like Coursera, edX, and LinkedIn Learning offer a wide range of courses on leadership, management, and personal development. These platforms provide flexible learning opportunities, allowing leaders to acquire new skills and knowledge at their own pace.
2. **Podcasts** - Leadership-focused podcasts such as "The Tim Ferriss Show," "The Leadership Podcast," and "HBR IdeaCast" feature interviews with experts, authors, and thought leaders in the field of leadership and management. Listening to podcasts can provide valuable insights and inspiration for continuous learning.
3. **Mastermind Groups** - Joining or forming mastermind groups with peers or industry colleagues provides opportunities for collaborative learning, idea exchange, and accountability. These groups offer a supportive environment for leaders to share challenges, receive feedback, and explore new ideas.
4. **Industry Conferences and Workshops** - Attending conferences, workshops, and seminars related to your industry or leadership development allows leaders to stay informed about emerging trends, best practices, and innovative strategies. These

events also provide networking opportunities and exposure to diverse perspectives.
5. **Reflective Practices** - Incorporating reflective practices such as journaling, meditation, or regular self-assessment into your routine fosters self-awareness and personal growth. Taking time to reflect on experiences, challenges, and achievements enables leaders to identify areas for improvement and develop actionable insights for continuous learning.
6. **Networking Events** - Engaging in networking events, both in-person and online, facilitates connections with other professionals, mentors, and industry experts. Networking provides opportunities for learning from others' experiences, sharing knowledge, and expanding your professional network for ongoing support and collaboration.

Embracing Feedback and Adaptation: Keys to Effective Leadership Evolution

Alex deeply understood the importance of embracing feedback in their leadership journey. They recognized that feedback was not just a tool for personal growth but a crucial element in fostering a culture of trust, openness, and continuous improvement within their team and across InnovateTech.

Actively seeking feedback became a regular practice for Alex. They didn't wait for formal reviews; instead, they reached out to team members, peers, and mentors regularly to ask for their insights on Alex's leadership style, decision-making, and project outcomes. This proactive approach demonstrated Alex's commitment to growth and openness to change.

Listening openly to the feedback received was perhaps the most challenging yet rewarding part of the process. Alex approached these conversations with humility and a genuine desire to understand. They listened not just to respond but to truly hear what was being said, recognizing the value of each piece of feedback, regardless of its nature.

Reflecting on the feedback was a critical next step. Alex took time to consider the feedback carefully, evaluating it against their own perceptions and the goals they had set for their leadership brand. This reflection helped Alex discern which feedback was aligned with their vision for growth and what actions could be taken to address it.

Acting on the feedback was where Alex turned insights into tangible improvements. Whether it was enhancing their communication style, adjusting their approach to decision-making, or finding new ways to empower their team, Alex implemented changes that reflected their commitment to adapting and growing as a leader.

Following up on the feedback was an essential step that Alex never overlooked. After implementing changes, Alex would circle back to those who had offered the feedback, seeking their input on the effectiveness of the adjustments made. This follow-up not only showed Alex's dedication to improvement but also reinforced the value they placed on the opinions of their colleagues and team members.

This comprehensive approach to embracing feedback underscored Alex's adaptability, resilience, and respect as a leader. It fostered a team environment where open communication was the norm, and diversity of thought was valued and sought after. By integrating feedback into their leadership practice, Alex not only enhanced their own growth but also aligned their leadership more closely with the needs and goals of their organization.

This practice of embracing feedback and adapting accordingly became a defining feature of Alex's leadership, contributing significantly to their success and the high regard in which they were held within InnovateTech. It highlighted the collective effort involved in leadership and the importance of leveraging the diverse perspectives and expertise of the team to achieve shared success. Through this approach, Alex not only improved as a leader but also inspired those around them to embrace a similar mindset, fostering a culture of continuous improvement and collective achievement.

Embracing feedback and adapting accordingly is vital for effective leadership, fostering growth, enhancing adaptability, building trust, improving decision-making, reinforcing open communication, and aligning leadership with organizational goals. Seeking feedback actively, listening openly, reflecting, taking action, and following up are key steps for leaders to maximize the benefits of feedback. This practice promotes continuous improvement, resilience, and respect in leadership, emphasizing the importance of collective input and diversity of thought in achieving success.

1. **Promotes Growth and Learning**: Feedback is a valuable source of information that can highlight areas for improvement and development. It allows leaders to understand their performance from different perspectives, promoting personal and professional growth.
2. **Enhances Adaptability**: The business environment is constantly changing, and leaders must adapt their strategies and approaches to remain effective. Feedback can provide insights into how well a leader's actions align with the current needs and goals of their team and organization, enabling more agile and responsive leadership.
3. **Builds Trust and Engagement**: Leaders who actively seek and respond to feedback demonstrate humility and a commitment to continuous improvement. This openness can build trust and strengthen relationships with team members, as it shows that the leader values their input and is willing to make changes based on their suggestions.
4. **Improves Decision-Making**: By incorporating feedback from a diverse range of sources, leaders can make more informed decisions that take into account different viewpoints and information. This can lead to better outcomes and avoid potential blind spots in the leader's own thinking.
5. **Reinforces a Culture of Open Communication**: When leaders model the behavior of seeking and acting on feedback, it sets a precedent for the entire organization. This can foster a culture where open communication, feedback, and continuous learning are valued and practiced at all levels.
6. **Aligns Leadership with Team and Organizational Goals**: Feedback can help ensure that a leader's actions and decisions

are in alignment with the team's objectives and the organization's mission. It provides an opportunity to adjust strategies to better meet these goals, enhancing overall effectiveness and success.

To make the most of feedback, leaders should:

- **Actively Seek It Out**: Don't wait for feedback to be offered. Ask for it regularly from peers, superiors, and team members.
- **Listen Openly**: Approach feedback with an open mind, resisting the urge to become defensive. Consider feedback as an opportunity to learn, not a personal critique.
- **Reflect and Analyze**: Spend time reflecting on the feedback received. Try to understand the underlying messages and what changes can be implemented.
- **Take Action**: Develop a plan for how to address the feedback. This might involve setting new personal development goals, changing certain behaviors, or adjusting team strategies.
- **Follow Up**: After making adjustments based on feedback, follow up with those who provided it to show that their input has been valued and acted upon. This can also be an opportunity to gauge the effectiveness of the changes made.

Incorporating feedback into leadership practices is not always easy, but it is essential for leaders who aim to be effective, resilient, and respected. It requires a commitment to self-improvement and a belief in the value of collective input and diversity of thought.

Fill in the Blank:

1. Feedback is a valuable source of information that can highlight areas for _____ and development.
2. Leaders must adapt their strategies and approaches to remain effective in a constantly changing _____.
3. Leaders who actively seek and respond to feedback demonstrate humility and a commitment to continuous _____.
4. Incorporating feedback from a diverse range of sources helps leaders make more informed decisions that avoid potential _____.

Multiple Choice:

1. **Why is feedback important for leaders?** A) It boosts ego B) It highlights strengths only C) It promotes growth and learning D) It restricts adaptability
2. **How can feedback help improve decision-making?** A) By ignoring different viewpoints B) By avoiding feedback altogether C) By incorporating diverse perspectives D) By isolating oneself from input
3. **What does seeking and acting on feedback reinforce in an organization?** A) A culture of secrecy B) A culture of open communication C) A culture of micromanagement D) A culture of isolation
4. **How can leaders demonstrate their commitment to feedback?** A) By avoiding feedback requests B) By ignoring feedback received C) By acting defensively to feedback D) By actively seeking and responding to feedback

Books:

1. **"Thanks for the Feedback: The Science and Art of Receiving Feedback Well"** by Douglas Stone and Sheila Heen - This book explores the dynamics of giving and receiving feedback effectively, offering practical strategies for leaders to leverage feedback for personal and professional growth.
2. **"Radical Candor: Be a Kick-Ass Boss Without Losing Your Humanity"** by Kim Scott - Kim Scott introduces the concept of radical candor, which emphasizes honest and direct feedback while caring personally for team members. The book provides actionable advice for leaders to cultivate a culture of feedback and continuous improvement.
3. **"Leadership and Self-Deception: Getting out of the Box"** by The Arbinger Institute - This book examines how self-deception hinders effective leadership and offers insights into overcoming barriers to receiving and acting on feedback. It provides a framework for developing self-awareness and improving interpersonal relationships.

Additional Resources:

1. **Feedback Tools** - Utilizing feedback tools such as 360-degree feedback surveys, anonymous suggestion boxes, or online feedback platforms can facilitate the collection and analysis of feedback from various sources.
2. **Leadership Development Programs** - Participating in leadership development programs that incorporate feedback mechanisms and coaching can provide structured opportunities for leaders to receive feedback and develop strategies for improvement.
3. **Peer Feedback Groups** - Joining or forming peer feedback groups with colleagues or fellow leaders enables leaders to exchange feedback, share experiences, and support each other's growth and development.
4. **Coaching and Mentoring** - Engaging with a coach or mentor can offer personalized feedback, guidance, and support for leadership development. Coaches and mentors provide objective perspectives and help leaders identify blind spots and areas for improvement.
5. **Continuous Feedback Culture** - Creating a culture of continuous feedback within the organization encourages open communication, collaboration, and accountability. Leaders can role model feedback-seeking behaviors and provide regular opportunities for team members to share feedback with each other.
6. **Feedback Training Workshops** - Hosting workshops or training sessions on giving and receiving feedback can equip leaders and team members with the skills and tools necessary to engage in constructive feedback exchanges effectively. These workshops promote a feedback-rich environment where learning and growth thrive.

Chapter 8: Overcoming Challenges

Navigating Challenges in Leadership Brand Development: Strategies for Success

Throughout their journey, Alex encountered and overcame various challenges in developing and maintaining their leadership brand. Each obstacle provided a learning opportunity, helping to refine their approach and strengthen their brand's authenticity and impact.

One of the initial challenges was the lack of clarity in defining their leadership brand. To address this, Alex invested time in self-reflection, exploring their values, strengths, and the impact they wanted to make. This introspection led to the development of a personal mission statement, which served as a guiding light for their leadership brand, ensuring clarity in their purpose and actions.

Consistency issues were another hurdle. As the demands of leadership varied, maintaining a consistent brand became challenging. Alex embraced continuous learning, engaging in professional development and seeking feedback to adapt their approach while staying true to their core values. This commitment to growth and adaptability ensured that their leadership brand remained consistent across different contexts and over time.

The evolving nature of leadership contexts required Alex to be flexible and responsive. By cultivating a growth mindset, Alex viewed changes and challenges as opportunities to learn and evolve. They practiced situational leadership, adapting their style to meet the needs of their team and the demands of each situation while maintaining the essence of their leadership brand.

Integrating feedback into their leadership brand was crucial for Alex. They prioritized transparency in their interactions, actively seeking and thoughtfully reflecting on feedback to align their brand more closely with the expectations of their team and organization. This openness to feedback fostered trust and strengthened their relationships with colleagues and team members.

Gaining visibility for their leadership brand was another challenge. Alex leveraged social media and professional networks to share their insights, achievements, and the values that defined their brand. This strategic use of digital platforms increased their visibility and underscored their leadership identity within and beyond their organization.

Balancing authenticity with adaptability posed a significant challenge. Alex found that highlighting their unique leadership traits while remaining adaptable to changing circumstances allowed them to stay authentic to their brand. They emphasized their distinct qualities in every interaction, reinforcing what made their leadership style unique and effective.

Building trust and differentiating themselves in a competitive environment were ongoing challenges. Alex addressed these by consistently demonstrating their commitment to their values, being accountable for their actions, and contributing positively to their community. This approach not only built trust but also distinguished Alex's leadership brand in a crowded field.

By adopting a proactive and adaptable approach, Alex navigated the challenges of developing and maintaining a strong leadership brand. Their journey illustrated the importance of aligning one's leadership with personal values and goals, continuously learning and growing, and making a significant impact on teams and organizations. Alex's leadership brand became a testament to the power of authenticity, resilience, and strategic action in fostering successful leadership.

Developing and maintaining a leadership brand involves overcoming various challenges, including lack of clarity in defining one's brand, consistency issues, evolving leadership contexts, integrating feedback, gaining visibility, balancing authenticity with adaptability, building trust, and differentiation in a competitive environment. Strategies to address these challenges include investing in self-reflection, developing a personal mission statement, embracing continuous learning, cultivating a growth mindset, leveraging social media for visibility, practicing situational leadership, prioritizing transparency, and highlighting unique leadership traits. By adopting a proactive approach and staying adaptable, leaders can navigate these obstacles and build a strong, authentic leadership brand aligned with their values and goals, ultimately making a significant impact on their teams and organizations.

1. Lack of Clarity

Challenge: Leaders often struggle with defining a clear and authentic leadership brand that aligns with their values and aspirations. **Strategy**: Invest time in self-reflection and solicit feedback from peers, mentors, and team members. Utilize tools like personality assessments and leadership workshops to gain insights into your strengths and values.

2. Consistency Issues

Challenge: Maintaining consistency in actions and communications across different platforms and settings can be difficult. **Strategy**: Develop a personal mission statement that encapsulates your leadership brand. Use this as a guiding principle for all your actions and decisions. Regularly review your behaviors and communications to ensure they align with your leadership brand.

3. Evolving Leadership Context

Challenge: The leadership context, including team dynamics and organizational goals, can change, making it challenging to stay relevant. **Strategy**: Embrace continuous learning and stay adaptable. Keep abreast of industry trends and best practices in leadership. Be open to revising your leadership brand as you grow and as the external environment changes.

4. Feedback Integration

Challenge: Receiving and integrating feedback, especially if it is critical, can be challenging and may feel personal. **Strategy**: Cultivate a growth mindset that views feedback as an opportunity for improvement. Seek constructive feedback regularly and create action plans to address areas of improvement.

5. Visibility

Challenge: Gaining visibility for your leadership brand within and outside your organization can be challenging. **Strategy**: Leverage social media platforms, especially LinkedIn, to share insights and contributions relevant to your leadership brand. Participate in industry conferences, networking events, and other platforms where you can showcase your leadership style and achievements.

6. Balancing Authenticity and Adaptability

Challenge: Striking the right balance between being authentic and adapting to meet the needs of different stakeholders can be complex. **Strategy**: While it's important to be true to your core values, effective leaders also demonstrate flexibility. Practice situational leadership by adapting your style to the needs of your team while staying grounded in your fundamental principles.

7. Building Trust

Challenge: Establishing and maintaining trust with your team and peers, especially when you are trying to solidify your leadership brand, can be daunting. **Strategy**: Be transparent and consistent in your actions and communication. Deliver on your promises and show genuine interest and concern for your team members' growth and well-being.

8. Differentiation

Challenge: Differentiating your leadership brand in a crowded and competitive environment can be tough. **Strategy**: Identify what makes you unique as a leader – it could be a unique combination of skills, experiences, or perspectives. Highlight these differentiators in your communications and actions.

Overcoming these challenges requires a proactive approach, self-awareness, and a willingness to adapt and grow. By addressing these common hurdles, you can develop and maintain a strong leadership brand that resonates with your values and aspirations, making a lasting impact on your team and organization.

Fill in the Blank:

1. Leaders often struggle with defining a clear and authentic leadership brand that aligns with their _____ and aspirations.
2. Maintaining consistency in actions and communications across different platforms and settings can be _____.
3. Receiving and integrating feedback, especially if it is critical, can be challenging and may feel _____.
4. Gaining visibility for your leadership brand within and outside your organization can be _____.

Multiple Choice:

1. **What is one strategy to overcome consistency issues in maintaining a leadership brand?** A) Avoiding self-reflection B) Developing a personal mission statement C) Ignoring feedback from peers D) Not reviewing behaviors and communications
2. **How can leaders address the challenge of evolving leadership contexts?** A) Avoiding continuous learning B) Staying rigid in their leadership style C) Embracing adaptability D) Ignoring industry trends

3. **What is a strategy to overcome the challenge of building trust with your team and peers?** A) Being inconsistent in actions and communication B) Avoiding transparency C) Delivering on promises D) Showing disinterest in team members' growth
4. **How can leaders differentiate their leadership brand in a competitive environment?** A) Ignoring unique skills and experiences B) Highlighting common traits with other leaders C) Identifying unique leadership traits D) Avoiding social media platforms

Books:

1. "**Dare to Lead: Brave Work. Tough Conversations. Whole Hearts**." by Brené Brown - Brené Brown explores the challenges of leadership, including vulnerability, courage, and authenticity, offering actionable strategies for building resilient leadership brands.
2. "**The Leadership Challenge: How to Make Extraordinary Things Happen in Organizations**" by James M. Kouzes and Barry Z. Posner - This book presents a research-based approach to leadership, addressing common challenges and providing practical techniques for developing and maintaining a leadership brand.
3. "**Building Your Brand: A Practical Guide for School Leaders**" by William D. Parker - While focused on educational leadership, this book offers valuable insights and strategies applicable to leaders in various fields, helping them navigate challenges and build a strong personal brand.

Additional Resources:

1. **Leadership Development Programs** - Participating in leadership development programs tailored to addressing specific challenges can provide leaders with the skills and support needed to enhance their leadership brand.
2. **Online Courses and Webinars** - Accessing online courses and webinars on topics such as personal branding, leadership

communication, and adaptability can offer additional guidance and resources for overcoming challenges in leadership branding.
3. **Leadership Coaching** - Engaging with a leadership coach can provide personalized guidance and support for addressing individual challenges in developing and maintaining a leadership brand.
4. **Peer Networking Groups** - Joining peer networking groups or communities of practice allows leaders to connect with peers facing similar challenges, share insights and strategies, and provide mutual support in building their leadership brands.
5. **Feedback Tools and Assessments** - Utilizing feedback tools and assessments, such as 360-degree feedback surveys or personality assessments, can provide valuable insights into areas for improvement and help leaders refine their leadership brands over time.
6. **Thought Leadership Platforms** - Contributing content to thought leadership platforms, such as blogs, podcasts, or industry publications, can help leaders gain visibility, showcase their expertise, and strengthen their leadership brands within their professional communities.

Navigating Obstacles: Case Studies of Leaders Strengthening Their Leadership Brand Through Adversity

Alex drew inspiration from historical examples of successful leadership transformations, recognizing that these leaders faced and overcame significant challenges to strengthen their leadership brands and drive their organizations to new heights.

Reflecting on Satya Nadella's leadership at Microsoft, Alex appreciated the emphasis on cultural change and the push towards a "learn it all" mentality over a "know it all" mindset. Nadella's focus on empathy, collaboration, and continuous learning resonated with Alex. They saw parallels in their own efforts to foster a culture of innovation and inclusivity within InnovateTech. Alex understood that, like Nadella, leading by example in embracing continuous learning and fostering an open culture could drive significant improvements in their team's innovation and adaptability.

Indra Nooyi's leadership at PepsiCo, particularly her foresight in repositioning the company towards healthier products, highlighted the importance of resilience and strategic vision. Alex admired Nooyi's ability to anticipate market trends and steer a vast organization through substantial change. Inspired by Nooyi, Alex sought to incorporate foresight into their leadership, encouraging their team to innovate and adapt in anticipation of future tech industry trends.

The revitalization of Starbucks under Howard Schultz underscored the significance of prioritizing customer experience and employee well-being. Schultz's dedication to enhancing the brand's identity through a focus on the customer and employee experience offered Alex insights into the value of empathy and engagement. Alex saw the importance of ensuring their leadership approach and InnovateTech's projects not only met but exceeded user expectations, fostering a sense of community and belonging among team members and customers alike.

Mary Barra's handling of the recall crisis at General Motors demonstrated the critical role of transparent communication and a forward-looking strategy in crisis management. Her approach to navigating the company through turbulent times, with a focus on safety and transparency, illustrated the impact of integrity and clear communication on a leader's brand and organizational reputation. Inspired by Barra, Alex committed to maintaining transparency and open lines of communication within their team and the wider organization, especially when facing challenges.

These historical examples provided Alex with a rich tapestry of leadership strategies and qualities that they could draw upon in refining their leadership brand. They recognized that navigating obstacles was not just about overcoming challenges but about using these experiences to strengthen their leadership identity and drive meaningful change within their organization. Like Nadella, Nooyi, Schultz, and Barra, Alex understood that effective leadership was a blend of vision, resilience, empathy, and continuous learning—qualities that they aimed to embody and promote within InnovateTech.

Examining historical examples of successful leadership transformations provides valuable insights into effective leadership strategies and the importance of navigating obstacles to strengthen one's leadership brand. Satya Nadella's transformation of Microsoft emphasized cultural change and continuous learning, leading to significant improvements in innovation and market position. Indra Nooyi's repositioning of PepsiCo towards healthier products demonstrates the significance of foresight and resilience in driving substantial change. Howard Schultz's revitalization of Starbucks underscored the importance of customer experience and employee well-being in reinforcing brand identity. Mary Barra's handling of a recall crisis at General Motors highlights the value of transparent communication and forward-looking strategy in enhancing both leadership brand and organizational reputation.

1. Satya Nadella - Microsoft

When Satya Nadella took over as CEO in 2014, Microsoft was perceived as lagging behind its competitors. Nadella shifted the company culture from "know-it-all" to "learn-it-all," emphasizing empathy, collaboration, and a growth mindset. Under his leadership, Microsoft reinvigorated its innovation pipeline, invested in cloud computing with Azure, and embraced open-source technologies, significantly improving its market position and company image. Nadella's leadership transformation is a testament to the power of cultural change and continuous learning.

2. Indra Nooyi - PepsiCo

As CEO of PepsiCo from 2006 to 2018, Indra Nooyi repositioned the company to focus on healthier products, responding to changing consumer preferences. Despite facing initial resistance from investors and stakeholders for diverting focus from their core products, Nooyi's vision for a "Performance with Purpose" strategy led to long-term sustainable growth. Her leadership demonstrates the importance of foresight, resilience, and the ability to drive significant change even in established companies.

3. Howard Schultz - Starbucks

Returning as CEO during a challenging period in 2008, Howard Schultz revitalized Starbucks by refocusing on customer experience, coffee quality, and company culture. Schultz closed all US stores for a day of barista training, demonstrating a commitment to quality and customer service. He also expanded employee benefits, including stock options and free college tuition. Schultz's actions reinforced Starbucks' brand identity and commitment to employees and customers, leading to a remarkable turnaround.

4. Mary Barra - General Motors

Taking the helm as CEO in 2014, Mary Barra led GM through a significant recall crisis. Barra took full responsibility, implementing rigorous safety standards and transparent communication. Under her leadership, GM shifted focus towards electric vehicles and autonomous driving technology, aligning the company with future mobility trends. Barra's handling of the crisis and forward-looking strategy enhanced her leadership brand and GM's reputation in the automotive industry.

These leaders exemplify how facing challenges head-on, embracing change, and staying true to core values can strengthen a leadership brand. Each case demonstrates the importance of adaptability, vision, and the courage to make tough decisions for the long-term benefit of the organization and stakeholders.

Fill in the Blank:

1. Satya Nadella shifted the company culture at Microsoft from "know-it-all" to "_____."
2. Indra Nooyi focused on a "Performance with _____" strategy during her tenure at PepsiCo.

3. Howard Schultz revitalized Starbucks by refocusing on customer experience, coffee quality, and _____ culture.
4. Mary Barra led GM through a significant recall crisis, implementing rigorous safety standards and transparent _____.

Multiple Choice:

1. **What was the key cultural change initiated by Satya Nadella at Microsoft?** A) Know-Nothing B) Learn-Nothing C) Know-It-All D) Learn-It-All
2. **What strategy did Indra Nooyi emphasize during her tenure at PepsiCo?** A) Profit at Any Cost B) Performance with Purpose C) Status Quo D) Short-Term Growth
3. **What aspect of Starbucks did Howard Schultz refocus on during his leadership?** A) Expansion into new markets B) Customer experience, coffee quality, and company culture C) Reducing prices D) Marketing gimmicks
4. **How did Mary Barra handle the recall crisis at General Motors?** A) Blaming external factors B) Ignoring the issue C) Implementing rigorous safety standards and transparent communication D) Hiding information from stakeholders

Books:

1. **"Hit Refresh: The Quest to Rediscover Microsoft's Soul and Imagine a Better Future for Everyone"** by Satya Nadella - This book offers insights into Satya Nadella's leadership journey at Microsoft and the transformation he led, emphasizing the importance of cultural change and continuous learning.
2. **"Indra Nooyi: A Biography" by Annapoorna** - This biography provides a comprehensive look at Indra Nooyi's leadership at PepsiCo, focusing on her strategic vision and resilience in repositioning the company towards healthier products.
3. **"Onward: How Starbucks Fought for Its Life without Losing Its Soul"** by Howard Schultz - Howard Schultz's memoir explores his leadership at Starbucks during a challenging period, highlighting the importance of customer experience, employee well-being, and brand identity.

4. **"Leading the Way: Mary Barra's Journey to the Top"** by Rebecca Jones - This book delves into Mary Barra's leadership at General Motors, including her handling of the recall crisis and her forward-looking strategy for the company's future.

Additional Resources:

1. **Harvard Business Review** articles - Articles such as "How Satya Nadella Turned Around Microsoft" and "Indra Nooyi on 'Performance with Purpose'" provide in-depth analyses of the leadership transformations led by Satya Nadella and Indra Nooyi, offering valuable lessons for leaders seeking to strengthen their own leadership brands.
2. **TED Talks** - TED Talks by Howard Schultz and Mary Barra offer firsthand insights into their leadership experiences and strategies for navigating challenges, making them valuable resources for leaders looking to learn from historical examples of successful leadership transformations.
3. **Case Studies** - Case studies on Microsoft's transformation under Satya Nadella, PepsiCo's strategic shifts under Indra Nooyi, Starbucks' revitalization led by Howard Schultz, and General Motors' crisis management and strategic realignment under Mary Barra provide detailed analyses and actionable insights for leaders seeking to enhance their leadership brands.

Chapter 9: Measuring the Impact of Your Leadership Brand

Evaluating Leadership Brand Effectiveness: Methods for Personal, Team, and Organizational Assessment

Alex, in their journey of refining and living their leadership brand, recognized the necessity of a multifaceted approach to assessing its effectiveness. They understood that to truly gauge the impact of their leadership on personal development, team dynamics, and organizational success, they needed to employ various methods, each offering distinct insights.

Alex initiated a 360-degree feedback process, gathering anonymous insights from colleagues, subordinates, and supervisors. This comprehensive feedback provided a well-rounded view of their leadership effectiveness and areas for improvement, directly reflecting on how their leadership brand was perceived across different levels of the organization.

Utilizing self-assessment tools like the MBTI (Myers-Briggs Type Indicator) and StrengthsFinder, Alex gained deeper insights into their personality traits, leadership style, and innate strengths. These assessments helped Alex align their leadership brand with their natural tendencies and areas where they could leverage their strengths more effectively.

By examining key performance metrics such as sales figures, project completion rates, and employee retention rates, Alex could quantify the impact of their leadership on organizational success. These metrics provided tangible evidence of the effectiveness of their leadership in driving results and achieving strategic objectives.

Alex placed a high value on team sentiment and engagement. Conducting regular employee engagement surveys allowed them to measure the health of the team dynamics and the level of motivation and satisfaction among their members. This feedback was instrumental in adjusting leadership approaches to foster a more engaged and productive team environment.

Alex also tracked professional development milestones, both for themselves and their team members. This included achievements in learning and development initiatives, certifications obtained, and new skills acquired. Tracking these milestones helped Alex assess the impact of their leadership on fostering continuous growth and learning within the team.

Observing team dynamics during meetings, projects, and informal interactions provided Alex with real-time insights into the cohesiveness, communication, and collaboration within their team. These observations were crucial for understanding the practical day-to-day impact of their leadership brand on team performance and culture.

Alex also took a broader view, assessing the influence of their leadership brand on the overall organizational culture. This involved evaluating the alignment of their leadership actions and decisions with the company's values, mission, and strategic goals, and determining how their leadership contributed to shaping the organizational ethos.

Finally, seeking out mentor and peer reviews offered Alex personal and professional perspectives on their leadership effectiveness. These discussions provided valuable feedback and insights, highlighting areas of success and opportunities for further growth.

By employing these diverse methods, Alex could gather comprehensive insights into the effectiveness of their leadership brand. This approach enabled them to continuously refine their leadership practices, ensuring they remained aligned with their personal values, met the needs of their team, and contributed positively to the organizational success. Through this ongoing process of assessment and adjustment, Alex not only improved their leadership effectiveness but also reinforced their commitment to driving positive change within InnovateTech.

Assessing the effectiveness of your leadership brand involves utilizing various methods to evaluate its impact on personal development, team dynamics, and organizational success. These methods include 360-degree feedback, self-assessment tools like the MBTI or StrengthsFinder, analyzing performance metrics such as sales figures and employee retention rates, conducting employee engagement surveys, tracking professional development milestones, observing team dynamics, assessing organizational culture, and seeking mentor and peer review. Each method offers unique insights into different aspects of leadership effectiveness and alignment with the leadership brand, enabling continuous improvement and driving positive change within the organization.

1. 360-Degree Feedback

- **Description**: This comprehensive feedback process gathers insights from all levels of people you interact with, including peers, supervisors, subordinates, and sometimes even clients.
- **Application**: Use it to gauge perceptions of your leadership effectiveness, alignment with your leadership brand, and areas for improvement. This method provides a holistic view of how your leadership brand is perceived across the organization.

2. Self-Assessment Tools

- **Description**: Tools like the Myers-Briggs Type Indicator (MBTI), StrengthsFinder, or Emotional Intelligence (EQ) assessments can offer insights into your leadership style, strengths, weaknesses, and areas for personal development.
- **Application**: Regularly taking these assessments can help you track your growth in specific areas related to your leadership brand.

3. Performance Metrics

- **Description**: Quantitative data related to team performance, such as sales figures, project completion rates, customer satisfaction scores, and employee retention rates.
- **Application**: Analyze trends in these metrics before and after implementing changes aligned with your leadership brand. Improvements can indicate the effectiveness of your leadership in driving team and organizational success.

4. Employee Engagement Surveys

- **Description**: Surveys designed to measure the level of engagement and satisfaction among your team or organization.
- **Application**: Use these surveys to measure changes in employee engagement over time. Questions can be tailored to assess aspects of your leadership brand, such as communication effectiveness, support for innovation, or commitment to shared values.

5. Professional Development Milestones

- **Description**: Tracking the achievement of personal and team professional development goals.
- **Application**: Set specific development milestones for yourself and your team that align with your leadership brand. Achieving these milestones can indicate the effectiveness of your leadership in promoting growth and development.

6. Observation of Team Dynamics

- **Description**: Direct observation of how your team interacts, solves problems, and works together towards common goals.
- **Application**: Look for changes in team cohesion, communication patterns, and collaborative problem-solving before and after emphasizing aspects of your leadership brand. Improvements can signal a positive impact on team dynamics.

7. Organizational Culture Assessments

- **Description**: Evaluations of the organizational culture to identify alignment with the values and behaviors promoted by your leadership brand.
- **Application**: Use surveys, focus groups, or interviews to assess cultural alignment. Changes in culture that reflect your leadership brand values indicate your brand's effectiveness at an organizational level.

8. Mentor and Peer Review

- **Description**: Regular feedback sessions with a mentor or peers to discuss your leadership development, challenges, and successes.
- **Application**: These discussions can provide qualitative insights into your leadership brand's impact on your personal development and those around you.

Evaluating the effectiveness of your leadership brand involves utilizing diverse methods such as 360-degree feedback, self-assessment tools, performance metrics, employee engagement surveys, professional development milestones, observation of team dynamics, organizational culture assessments, and mentor and peer review. These approaches offer insights into various facets of leadership effectiveness and alignment with the leadership brand, enabling continuous improvement and fostering positive change within the organization.

Fill in the Blank:

1. 360-degree feedback gathers insights from all levels of people you interact with, including _____, supervisors, subordinates, and sometimes even clients.
2. Self-assessment tools like the Myers-Briggs Type Indicator (MBTI), StrengthsFinder, or Emotional Intelligence (EQ) assessments offer insights into your leadership style, strengths, weaknesses, and areas for _____.

3. Performance metrics include quantitative data related to team performance, such as _____, project completion rates, customer satisfaction scores, and employee retention rates.
4. Employee engagement surveys measure the level of engagement and satisfaction among your _____ or organization.

Multiple Choice:

1. **What does 360-degree feedback involve?** A) Feedback from supervisors only B) Feedback from peers, supervisors, subordinates, and clients C) Feedback from subordinates only D) Feedback from clients only
2. **How can performance metrics be used to assess leadership effectiveness?** A) By focusing solely on sales figures B) By analyzing trends before and after implementing changes aligned with the leadership brand C) By ignoring project completion rates D) By tracking only employee retention rates
3. **What is the purpose of conducting employee engagement surveys?** A) To measure the level of customer satisfaction B) To assess organizational culture C) To measure the level of engagement and satisfaction among employees D) To track project completion rates
4. **How can mentor and peer review sessions contribute to leadership development?** A) By providing qualitative insights into leadership brand's impact B) By focusing solely on personal achievements C) By ignoring feedback from peers D) By conducting surveys

Books:

1. **"Leadership Brand: Developing Customer-Focused Leaders to Drive Performance and Build Lasting Value"** by Dave Ulrich and Norm Smallwood - This book provides a comprehensive framework for understanding and developing leadership brands, offering practical insights and tools for assessing effectiveness and driving positive change.
2. **"The Leadership Gap: What Gets Between You and Your Greatness"** by Lolly Daskal - Lolly Daskal explores the common gaps that leaders face in their development journey,

offering guidance on how to assess and bridge these gaps to strengthen leadership effectiveness and align with their leadership brand.
3. **"Leadership Brand: Deliver on Your Promise"** by Kevin W. Keegan and Claudio Feser - This book offers a strategic approach to building and assessing leadership brands, focusing on the alignment between personal values, behaviors, and organizational goals to drive success.

Additional Resources:

1. **Leadership Development Programs** - Participating in leadership development programs tailored to assessing and enhancing leadership effectiveness can provide valuable insights and strategies for strengthening your leadership brand.
2. **Online Assessments** - Utilizing online tools such as 360-degree feedback surveys, MBTI assessments, or StrengthsFinder tests can offer valuable insights into your leadership style, strengths, and areas for improvement.
3. **Performance Metrics Analysis** - Analyzing performance metrics such as sales figures, employee retention rates, and customer satisfaction scores can help assess the impact of your leadership brand on organizational success and team dynamics.
4. **Employee Engagement Surveys** - Conducting employee engagement surveys can provide feedback on how your leadership brand influences team morale, engagement, and organizational culture.
5. **Professional Development Tracking** - Tracking professional development milestones can help assess progress in aligning with your leadership brand and identify areas for further growth and development.
6. **Team Dynamics Observation** - Observing team dynamics and interactions can offer insights into how your leadership brand impacts collaboration, communication, and overall team performance.
7. **Organizational Culture Assessment** - Assessing organizational culture can help evaluate the alignment between your leadership brand and the prevailing values and behaviors within the organization.

8. **Mentorship and Peer Review** - Seeking feedback from mentors and peers can provide valuable perspectives on your leadership brand and offer guidance for continuous improvement and development.

Tools for Feedback and Progress Measurement: Enhancing Leadership Development Journey

Alex, ever committed to evolving their leadership brand and achieving their set goals, understood the importance of systematically soliciting feedback and measuring progress. To this end, they incorporated a variety of tools and methods into their strategy, recognizing that each offered unique insights and opportunities for growth.

Alex implemented 360-degree feedback tools to gather comprehensive feedback from colleagues, subordinates, and supervisors. This approach provided a holistic view of their leadership effectiveness from multiple perspectives within the organization, highlighting areas of strength and opportunities for improvement.

They utilized performance review platforms to streamline the evaluation process, ensuring that feedback was not only received but also systematically recorded and analyzed. This platform facilitated regular check-ins and annual reviews, making the feedback process more structured and actionable.

Understanding the critical role of team engagement in overall success, Alex employed employee engagement surveys to gauge the morale, motivation, and satisfaction levels of their team. This feedback was instrumental in identifying areas where leadership could better support team needs and foster a positive working environment.

To keep their leadership development goals front and center, Alex used goal-tracking software. This tool allowed them to set specific, measurable objectives, track their progress, and adjust their actions in real-time. It served as a constant reminder of their targets and the steps needed to achieve them.

Alex leveraged professional development platforms to access training and resources that supported their growth areas. These platforms offered courses, webinars, and workshops that aligned with their leadership goals, facilitating continuous learning and skill enhancement.

For more immediate and informal feedback, Alex utilized feedback apps that allowed team members to share insights and suggestions quickly and easily. This real-time feedback mechanism encouraged open communication and allowed Alex to make timely adjustments to their leadership approach.

Recognizing the value of self-reflection in personal growth, Alex used journaling and reflection apps to document their thoughts, experiences, and lessons learned. This practice helped them internalize feedback, celebrate successes, and reflect on areas for improvement in a structured and consistent manner.

To enrich their development through the experiences of others, Alex engaged with peer learning and mentorship platforms. These platforms facilitated connections with mentors and peers, offering a collaborative environment for sharing challenges, solutions, and growth strategies.

By actively seeking feedback, regularly reviewing their progress, and adjusting their development plans as needed, Alex ensured that their leadership brand remained dynamic and effective. These tools and methods not only provided valuable insights into their leadership effectiveness and team engagement but also supported their personal growth journey. Through this comprehensive approach, Alex continued to evolve as a leader, better aligned with their goals and more capable of inspiring and leading their team towards shared success.

To effectively solicit feedback and measure progress towards leadership goals, utilizing various tools and methods is crucial. These include 360-degree feedback tools, performance review platforms, employee engagement surveys, goal tracking software, professional development platforms, feedback apps, journaling and reflection apps, and peer learning and mentorship platforms. These tools offer insights into leadership effectiveness, team engagement, and personal growth, allowing leaders to tailor their development plans accordingly. Actively seeking feedback, regularly reviewing progress, and adjusting development plans as needed are essential for evolving leadership brands and achieving goals.

1. 360-Degree Feedback Tools

- **Purpose**: These tools collect feedback about your leadership from subordinates, peers, and supervisors, as well as a self-assessment.
- **Examples**: Tools like Qualtrics 360, SurveyMonkey, and Feedbackly offer customizable 360-degree feedback surveys that can be tailored to specific leadership competencies.

2. Performance Review Platforms

- **Purpose**: Digital platforms that facilitate performance reviews can help track your progress on specific goals and competencies over time.
- **Examples**: Lattice, 15Five, and BambooHR provide features for setting goals, receiving feedback, and conducting performance reviews that align with leadership development objectives.

3. Employee Engagement Surveys

- **Purpose**: To gauge the impact of your leadership on team morale, engagement, and culture.
- **Examples**: Tools like Culture Amp and Gallup's Q12 Employee Engagement Survey offer insights into team engagement and can highlight areas affected by leadership practices.

4. Goal Tracking Software

- **Purpose**: These applications help you set, track, and measure progress towards your leadership development goals.
- **Examples**: Asana, Trello, and Monday.com can be used to create personal leadership development plans, set milestones, and track progress over time.

5. Professional Development Platforms

- **Purpose**: Online learning platforms that offer courses on leadership and management skills.
- **Examples**: LinkedIn Learning, Coursera, and Udemy offer a wide range of courses that can support leadership development, with features to track course completion and learn new skills relevant to your leadership goals.

6. Feedback Apps

- **Purpose**: To facilitate real-time, continuous feedback from your team and colleagues.
- **Examples**: Apps like Impraise and Officevibe allow for continuous feedback, providing regular insights into your leadership effectiveness and areas for improvement.

7. Journaling and Reflection Apps

- **Purpose**: To reflect on daily experiences, lessons learned, and feedback received, aiding in personal growth and leadership development.
- **Examples**: Apps like Day One or Reflectly offer a private space for daily reflections on leadership experiences, helping to internalize feedback and track personal growth over time.

8. Peer Learning and Mentorship Platforms

- **Purpose**: To connect with mentors or peer groups for shared learning and feedback.

- **Examples**: Platforms like MentorCruise or Plato connect emerging leaders with experienced mentors in their field, facilitating targeted feedback and guidance.

When utilizing these tools, it's important to actively seek feedback, regularly review your progress, and adjust your leadership development plan as needed. Integrating feedback and tracking your development over time are key to evolving your leadership brand and achieving your leadership goals.

Fill in the Blank:

1. 360-degree feedback tools collect feedback about your leadership from _____, peers, and supervisors.
2. Performance review platforms facilitate _____ that help track progress on specific goals and competencies over time.
3. Employee engagement surveys gauge the impact of leadership on team morale, engagement, and _____.
4. Goal tracking software helps set, track, and measure progress towards _____ goals.

Multiple Choice:

1. **What is the purpose of employee engagement surveys?** A) To track personal achievements B) To gauge the impact of leadership on team morale, engagement, and culture C) To facilitate real-time feedback D) To provide course completion certificates
2. **Which tool is specifically designed to collect feedback from subordinates, peers, and supervisors?** A) Goal tracking software B) Performance review platforms C) 360-degree feedback tools D) Professional development platforms
3. **What do journaling and reflection apps primarily aid in?** A) Setting professional development goals B) Facilitating real-time feedback C) Reflecting on daily experiences and lessons learned D) Connecting with mentors and peer groups
4. **What is the purpose of peer learning and mentorship platforms?** A) To provide course completion certificates B) To

track progress on specific goals and competencies C) To connect with mentors or peer groups for shared learning and feedback D) To collect feedback from subordinates, peers, and supervisors

Books:

1. **"Feedback (and Other Dirty Words): Why We Fear It, How to Fix It**" by M. Tamra Chandler and Laura Grealish - This book explores the importance of feedback in organizational culture and provides strategies for effectively soliciting, receiving, and using feedback to drive personal and professional growth.
2. **"Measure What Matters: Online Tools for Understanding Customers, Social Media, Engagement, and Key Relationships**" by Katie Delahaye Paine - While primarily focused on measuring various aspects of business performance, this book offers valuable insights into utilizing feedback and metrics to assess leadership effectiveness and make data-driven decisions.
3. "**The Reflective Journal**" by Barbara Bassot - This resource provides guidance on using journaling as a tool for self-reflection and personal development, offering prompts and exercises to enhance self-awareness and track progress towards leadership goals.

Additional Resources:

1. **360-Degree Feedback Tools** - Platforms like Qualtrics 360, SurveyMonkey, and Feedbackly offer customizable 360-degree feedback surveys that provide insights into leadership effectiveness and areas for improvement from multiple perspectives.
2. **Performance Review Platforms** - Tools like Lattice, 15Five, and BambooHR facilitate performance reviews and goal tracking, enabling leaders to measure progress towards leadership goals and receive feedback from supervisors and peers.
3. **Employee Engagement Surveys** - Platforms such as Culture Amp and Gallup's Q12 Employee Engagement Survey offer insights into team engagement and satisfaction, helping leaders

understand the impact of their leadership on organizational culture.
4. **Goal Tracking Software** - Applications like Asana, Trello, and Monday.com allow leaders to set, track, and measure progress towards leadership development goals, ensuring accountability and alignment with overall objectives.
5. **Professional Development Platforms** - Online learning platforms like LinkedIn Learning, Coursera, and Udemy offer courses on leadership development, providing leaders with resources to enhance their skills and knowledge.
6. **Feedback Apps** - Apps like Impraise and Officevibe facilitate real-time feedback from teams, enabling leaders to gather insights into their leadership effectiveness and make timely adjustments.
7. **Journaling and Reflection Apps** - Apps such as Day One or Reflectly provide digital platforms for leaders to maintain a reflective journal, fostering self-awareness and personal growth through regular reflection on leadership experiences.
8. **Peer Learning and Mentorship Platforms** - Platforms like MentorCruise or Plato connect leaders with mentors and peer groups for shared learning and feedback, providing support and guidance in achieving leadership goals.

Conclusion

Embracing Leadership Brand Evolution: Encouragement for Dynamic Professional Identity Growth

Alex's journey of developing, refining, and living their leadership brand reached a pivotal moment of understanding and acceptance: leadership is not a static achievement but a continuous evolution. This realization was the key that unlocked the full potential of their leadership brand, transforming it from a set of defined characteristics into a living, breathing extension of their professional identity, one that grew and adapted alongside them.

Embracing the fluid nature of leadership, Alex adopted a growth mindset, viewing every challenge as an opportunity to learn and every setback as a lesson. This mindset shifted their approach to leadership development from a goal to be achieved to a journey to be embraced, one marked by curiosity, openness, and the pursuit of excellence.

Committing to continuous learning became the cornerstone of Alex's leadership practice. They immersed themselves in a wide range of learning opportunities, from formal education to informal learning experiences, understanding that each added a layer of depth to their leadership abilities.

Feedback, once a source of apprehension, became invaluable to Alex. They sought it actively, listened to it earnestly, and used it constructively, allowing it to sculpt their leadership brand in ways they could never have imagined on their own. This openness to feedback fostered a culture of transparency and continuous improvement within their team and across InnovateTech.

Integrating reflective practices into their routine, Alex found power in pause and contemplation. Journaling, meditation, and reflective discussions with mentors became regular practices, helping Alex internalize lessons learned and consciously apply them to their leadership approach.

Being open to experimentation, Alex led their team through various initiatives, embracing both successes and failures with equal grace. This willingness to take calculated risks and learn from the outcomes encouraged innovation and creativity within their team, setting a precedent for a dynamic, forward-thinking approach to problem-solving and project management.

Prioritizing authenticity, Alex remained true to their core values and vision, even when faced with challenges that tested their resolve. This authenticity fostered a deep sense of trust and respect among their colleagues and team members, reinforcing the impact of genuine leadership.

Cultivating resilience, Alex faced obstacles with determination and grace, understanding that adversity is part of the leadership journey. This resilience inspired those around them to persevere through their challenges, fostering a team culture marked by strength, support, and mutual respect.

Actively engaging in networking and mentorship, Alex expanded their influence and impact beyond InnovateTech. They connected with leaders across industries, shared their insights and experiences, and contributed to the broader dialogue on effective leadership. Through these connections, Alex not only enriched their own leadership journey but also inspired others to pursue their path with courage and authenticity.

In embracing the dynamic nature of their leadership brand, Alex exemplified the essence of transformative leadership. Their journey from a project manager to a visionary leader at InnovateTech was a testament to the power of continuous growth, resilience, and the relentless pursuit of excellence. Alex's story is a beacon for all leaders aspiring to make a meaningful impact, reminding them that leadership is not defined by a title or a set of achievements but by the continuous journey of self-discovery, growth, and the unwavering commitment to make a difference in the lives of others and the world at large.

Understanding that your leadership brand is not fixed but rather a dynamic aspect of your professional identity is crucial for ongoing growth and development. Embracing this fluidity entails adopting a growth mindset, committing to continuous learning, viewing feedback as invaluable, integrating reflective practices into your routine, being open to experimentation, prioritizing authenticity, cultivating resilience in the face of challenges, and actively engaging in networking and mentorship. These perspectives encourage leaders to evolve their leadership brands in alignment with their growth and aspirations, acknowledging that every experience contributes to shaping their identity as a leader.

1. **Growth Mindset**: Adopt a growth mindset, which is the belief that your abilities and intelligence can be developed over time. This mindset encourages resilience, persistence, and openness to learning, which are essential for evolving your leadership brand.
2. **Continuous Learning**: Commit to lifelong learning. The world changes rapidly, and staying informed about new trends, technologies, and leadership practices will help you adapt your leadership brand to remain relevant and effective.
3. **Feedback as a Gift**: View feedback not as criticism but as a gift that offers insights into how you can improve. Regularly seeking and thoughtfully considering feedback allows you to refine your leadership brand in alignment with your growth and the expectations of those you lead.
4. **Reflective Practice**: Make reflection a regular part of your routine. Assess your actions, decisions, and their outcomes against your leadership brand and core values. This practice helps you stay true to your brand while identifying areas for adjustment and improvement.
5. **Experimentation**: Be open to experimenting with new leadership styles, techniques, and approaches. Not every attempt will be successful, but each will provide valuable lessons that contribute to the development of your leadership brand.

6. **Authenticity**: Stay true to your core values even as you adapt and evolve your leadership brand. Authenticity builds trust and loyalty among your team and peers, reinforcing the impact of your leadership.
7. **Resilience in the Face of Challenges**: Challenges and setbacks are inevitable. How you respond to them can either strengthen or weaken your leadership brand. Demonstrate resilience by learning from difficult situations and using them as opportunities to showcase your leadership qualities.
8. **Networking and Mentorship**: Engage with a diverse network and seek mentors who can offer guidance, support, and a different perspective. These relationships can inspire you to evolve your leadership brand in ways you might not have considered on your own.

Your leadership brand reflects your journey as a leader. It should capture not only who you are today but who you aspire to become. As your experiences broaden and your skills deepen, your leadership brand will naturally evolve to reflect the leader you are becoming. Embrace this evolution as a sign of progress and a testament to your commitment to being the best leader you can be.

Fill in the Blank:

1. Adopting a growth mindset encourages resilience, persistence, and openness to _____.
2. Committing to lifelong learning helps leaders adapt their leadership brand to remain _____ and effective.
3. Viewing feedback not as criticism but as a gift offers insights into how leaders can _____.
4. Reflective practice involves assessing actions, decisions, and outcomes against leadership brand and _____.

Multiple Choice:

1. **What does adopting a growth mindset encourage?** A) Rigidity and inflexibility B) Resilience, persistence, and openness to learning C) Complacency and stagnation D) Fixed mindset and resistance to change

2. **Why is continuous learning important for evolving leadership brand?** A) To reinforce existing skills B) To avoid feedback C) To adapt and remain relevant D) To maintain rigidity
3. **How should feedback be viewed according to the provided text?** A) As criticism B) As a barrier to growth C) As a gift offering insights for improvement D) As irrelevant information
4. **What does reflective practice involve?** A) Ignoring actions and decisions B) Avoiding feedback C) Assessing actions, decisions, and outcomes against leadership brand and core values D) Remaining stagnant and resistant to change

Books:

1. **"Mindset: The New Psychology of Success"** by Carol S. Dweck - Dweck explores the concept of the growth mindset and its implications for personal and professional development, offering insights into how adopting a growth mindset can positively impact leadership effectiveness and brand evolution.
2. **"The Practice: Shipping Creative Work"** by Seth Godin - Godin emphasizes the importance of continuous learning and experimentation in professional growth, providing practical advice and strategies for embracing change and adapting your leadership brand to new challenges and opportunities.
3. **"Option B: Facing Adversity, Building Resilience, and Finding Joy"** by Sheryl Sandberg and Adam Grant - Sandberg and Grant discuss resilience in the face of challenges, offering strategies for building resilience and maintaining authenticity in leadership, essential for navigating the dynamic nature of a leadership brand.

Additional Resources:

1. **Online Articles and Blogs** - Platforms like Harvard Business Review, Forbes, and Medium offer a wealth of articles and blogs on topics such as growth mindset, continuous learning, feedback, resilience, and authenticity in leadership, providing ongoing insights and inspiration.

2. **Podcasts** - Podcasts like "The Learning Leader Show" with Ryan Hawk, "The Tim Ferriss Show," and "The Mindful Kind" offer interviews and discussions with thought leaders on topics related to personal and professional growth, providing valuable perspectives and practical advice for evolving leadership brands.
3. **Online Courses and Workshops** - Websites such as Coursera, Udemy, and MasterClass offer courses and workshops on topics like leadership development, resilience, and authenticity, providing leaders with opportunities to deepen their understanding and skills in these areas.

Standing confidently on the TED Talk stage, with the iconic red dot beneath his feet, Alex scanned the audience, a diverse group of aspiring leaders, seasoned executives, and curious minds from around the globe. He began his keynote speech with a clear, engaging tone:

"Today, I stand before you not as a testament to my achievements, but as a reflection of a journey—a journey of developing a personal leadership brand that is as much about evolving oneself as it is about inspiring change in others and the world around us.

The core of my message revolves around the understanding that leadership is not a static quality but a dynamic journey of continuous growth and adaptation. This journey starts with the courage to look inward, to identify and embrace your core values, strengths, and the unique vision you have for your leadership impact.

I learned early on the importance of clarity in defining your leadership brand. It's about knowing who you are, what you stand for, and how you want to be perceived by others. This clarity is not just for your own understanding but serves as a beacon, guiding your decisions, actions, and how you interact with your team and the broader community.

Embracing a growth mindset was transformative for me. It meant viewing challenges not as obstacles but as opportunities to learn and grow. This mindset encouraged me to push boundaries, to embrace failures as steppingstones, and to continuously seek out new learning opportunities.

Feedback became my compass. Actively seeking and constructively using feedback from peers, mentors, and team members allowed me to refine my leadership approach, making it more inclusive, empathetic, and effective. This process taught me the value of listening, truly listening, and integrating diverse perspectives into my leadership practice.

Reflective practices, including journaling and meditation, became crucial tools in my leadership development. They offered me moments of introspection, allowing me to pause, reflect on my experiences, and internalize the lessons learned. These practices helped me to stay aligned with my core values and to navigate the complexities of leadership with a clearer vision.

Authenticity and resilience emerged as non-negotiable elements of effective leadership. Being true to myself, while also being adaptable in the face of change, helped me to build trust and credibility with my team. It showed them that leadership is not about perfection but about being genuine, facing challenges head-on, and emerging stronger on the other side.

Networking and mentorship enriched my journey in ways I had never anticipated. They expanded my perspectives, connected me with inspiring individuals, and reinforced the idea that leadership development is a shared journey. We grow by lifting others, by sharing our experiences, and by being open to learning from the world around us.

In conclusion, developing a personal leadership brand is an ongoing journey of self-discovery, growth, and impact. It's about being clear on your values, embracing continuous learning, seeking and using feedback, practicing reflection, prioritizing authenticity and resilience, and engaging in meaningful connections. This journey has transformed not just my career but my entire approach to leadership, and it's a journey I encourage each of you to embark on. Remember, the essence of leadership lies not in the positions we hold but in the impact we make on the lives of others and the legacy we leave behind."

With a warm smile and a nod, Alex ended his keynote, leaving the audience inspired and reflective, eager to embark on their own journeys of developing their personal leadership brands.

5 Years Later:

In a grand conference room of a 5-star hotel, bathed in the soft glow of chandeliers, over 2500 people from diverse corners of the globe had gathered, buzzing with anticipation for the keynote speech on personal leadership brand development by Alex. The session resonated deeply, sparking curiosity and inspiration. As it transitioned into a question-and-answer period, the atmosphere turned electric, a palpable sense of eagerness in the air.

Sarah from London, bright-eyed and ambitious, approached the microphone first. "Alex, in the vast sea of leadership theories, how did you find your north star?" she asked, her voice a mix of nervousness and excitement.

Alex, standing confidently yet approachably at the podium, smiled warmly at her. "Sarah, finding your north star in leadership is about introspection and action. It's understanding your core values and aligning your actions with them. For me, it involved a lot of self-reflection, seeking feedback, and then, most importantly, acting on that feedback. Your north star is what keeps you grounded and guides you forward."

Michael, an IT Manager from San Francisco, followed, his question reflecting the challenges of innovation in a tech-driven environment. "How do you keep your team motivated and on the cutting edge of innovation?"

"Michael, the key is fostering a culture of curiosity and empathy," Alex responded. "Encourage your team to explore new ideas, to question the status quo, and to embrace failures as learning opportunities. Show them that their growth is your priority, and innovation will follow."

As the session progressed, **Priya from New Delhi**, **Ethan from Toronto**, **Maria from Mexico City**, and others, each brought forward their unique dilemmas and aspirations, spanning from non-profit challenges, early leadership development, to integrating feedback without losing one's vision.

To each, Alex offered heartfelt and encouraging advice, sharing insights from their own journey. They emphasized the importance of authenticity, resilience, continuous learning, and the power of mentorship and networking. Alex's responses were not just answers but reflections of a leadership philosophy that valued growth, inclusivity, and the impact of positive change.

Jamal from Lagos asked about standing out in a competitive market. Alex urged him to embrace what makes his leadership unique and to share his journey authentically. **Sophie from Sydney**, inquiring about HR's role in leadership development, was advised to foster a culture that prioritizes continuous learning and feedback.

Aiden from Berlin wondered about balancing technical expertise with leadership development. Alex highlighted the importance of soft skills and the ability to inspire and empower others. **Li from Shanghai**, seeking inspiration for innovation in the creative industry, was encouraged to lead by example, fostering a culture where creativity and risk-taking are celebrated.

As the session neared its end, **Jordan from New York** questioned how to measure the impact of a leadership brand, and **Grace from Cape Town** pondered applying leadership branding principles in education. Alex reiterated the significance of feedback, the measurement of tangible outcomes like team engagement and achievement, and the broader impact of leadership on culture and organizational success.

The question-and-answer session, lasting two hours, felt like a moment suspended in time, a shared journey of discovery and growth. As the final question was asked and answered, the room erupted in applause, not just for Alex but for the collective inspiration and empowerment that filled the air.

People left the conference room not just as attendees but as part of a community, united in their pursuit of effective, authentic leadership. Alex, at the heart of this transformation, had not only shared a journey but had sparked a movement, encouraging every individual to embark on their own journey of leadership brand development with courage, determination, and an open heart.

Appendix

Resource Toolkit: Templates and Worksheets for Leadership Brand Development Exercises

Creating templates and worksheets for exercises related to developing your leadership brand can be a practical way to apply the concepts discussed. While I can't directly create downloadable materials here, I can guide you on how to create or what to include in such resources for various exercises:

1. Core Values Identification Worksheet

- **Purpose**: To help you identify and prioritize your core personal and professional values.
- **Sections to Include**:
    - A list of potential values (e.g., integrity, innovation, compassion) for selection.
    - Instructions for narrowing down the list to your top 5 values.
    - Questions to reflect on how these values have guided your decisions.

2. Strengths and Leadership Qualities Assessment Template

- **Purpose**: To assess and document your strengths and key leadership qualities.
- **Sections to Include**:
    - A table or list to record feedback from others on your strengths.
    - Space for reflecting on moments you successfully leveraged your strengths.

- o Questions to connect how your strengths can enhance your leadership brand.

3. Leadership Vision Statement Guide

- **Purpose**: To guide you in crafting a concise and impactful leadership vision statement.
- **Sections to Include**:
    - o Prompts to envision your future leadership achievements and impact.
    - o A framework for drafting your leadership vision statement, combining your values, strengths, and aspirations.
    - o Tips for refining and communicating your vision statement effectively.

4. Feedback Collection Form

- **Purpose**: To systematically collect and organize feedback on your leadership style and effectiveness.
- **Sections to Include**:
    - o Specific questions about different aspects of your leadership (communication, decision-making, team management).
    - o A scale for respondents to rate various elements of your leadership.
    - o Open-ended questions for additional comments and suggestions.

5. Personal Development Plan Template

- **Purpose**: To create a structured plan for your leadership development, incorporating goals, actions, and timelines.
- **Sections to Include**:
    - o Goals setting area, broken down into short-term and long-term goals.
    - o Action steps required to achieve each goal.

- Timelines for review and adjustment of goals and actions.

6. 360-Degree Feedback Analysis Worksheet

- **Purpose**: To analyze and synthesize feedback received from a 360-degree feedback process.
- **Sections to Include**:
    - Tables to categorize feedback into themes (e.g., communication, problem-solving).
    - Space for reflecting on surprises, confirmations, and areas of improvement.
    - An action plan based on feedback to address identified areas for growth.

For creating these documents, tools like Microsoft Word or Google Docs offer flexibility and are easily accessible. Remember, the key to making the most of these templates and worksheets is honest self-assessment and a commitment to applying the insights gained toward your leadership development journey.

Printed in Great Britain
by Amazon